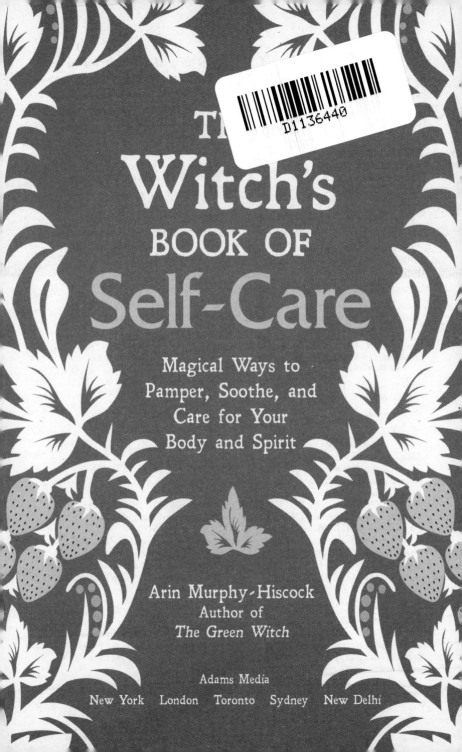

The
Witch's
BOOK OF
Self-Care

Magical Ways to
Pamper, Soothe, and
Care for Your
Body and Spirit

Arin Murphy-Hiscock
Author of
The Green Witch

Adams Media

New York   London   Toronto   Sydney   New Delhi

This one is for Ceri and Megan, who yell at me a lot in a caring way to not push myself beyond my limits and to stop feeling guilty for needing breaks. Back at you, ladies. I couldn't do this without you. Ice cream and spinning wheels forever.

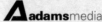

Adams Media
An Imprint of Simon & Schuster, Inc.
57 Littlefield Street
Avon, Massachusetts 02322

Copyright © 2018 by Simon & Schuster, Inc.

All rights reserved, including the right to reproduce this book or portions thereof in any form whatsoever. For information address Adams Media Subsidiary Rights Department, 1230 Avenue of the Americas, New York, NY 10020.

First Adams Media hardcover edition December 2018

ADAMS MEDIA and colophon are trademarks of Simon & Schuster, Inc.

For information about special discounts for bulk purchases, please contact Simon & Schuster Special Sales at 1-866-506-1949 or business@simonandschuster.com.

The Simon & Schuster Speakers Bureau can bring authors to your live event. For more information or to book an event contact the Simon & Schuster Speakers Bureau at 1-866-248-3049 or visit our website at www.simonspeakers.com.

Interior design by Katrina Machado
Interior images © Getty Images/kosmozoo

Printed and bound by CPI Group (UK) Ltd, Croydon, CR0 4YY

10 9 8 7

Library of Congress Cataloging-in-Publication Data
Murphy-Hiscock, Arin, author.
The witch's book of self-care / Arin Murphy-Hiscock, author of The Green Witch.
Avon, Massachusetts: Adams Media, 2018.
Includes bibliographical references and index.
LCCN 2018031996 | ISBN 9781507209141 (hc) | ISBN 9781507209158 (ebook)
Subjects: LCSH: Witchcraft. | Women--Health and hygiene. | Self-care, Health.
Classification: LCC BF1571.5.W66 M87 2018 | DDC 133.4/3--dc23
LC record available at https://urldefense.proofpoint.com/v2/url?u=https-3A__lccn
.loc.gov_2018031996&d=DwIFAg&c=jGUuvAdBXp_VqQ6t0yah2g&r=eLFfdQgpH-
VW0iSAzG8F-WtSjrFvCD9jGMJBHtzyExXhmHvwB7sjMCnFuKz95Uyqa&m=P6HIN-
5qAp_a4btALkY4IWULwe2ZzDJAuXVwuySuLLqg&s=SsoUAQ3VYDrgTfd3696rKH-
nAlUhDFpYCx2WeDMj2KTM&e=

ISBN 978-1-5072-1123-6
ISBN 978-1-5072-0915-8 (ebook)

Many of the designations used by manufacturers and sellers to distinguish their products are claimed as trademarks. Where those designations appear in this book and Simon & Schuster, Inc., was aware of a trademark claim, the designations have been printed with initial capital letters.

Contents

Acknowledgments

I would like to thank Rebecca Thomas for offering me the opportunity to write this book. It's a topic that is very dear to me, and even though my schedule was insane, I knew I had to write it!

I also want to acknowledge the teams at Ubisoft, Partworks, and Hachette for being so understanding; I juggled a ridiculous number of projects while I wrote this book. I appreciate your flexibility! I especially thank Anouk, who is also a warrior for self-care and defending personal time and energy while spinning an incredible number of plates. You're an inspiration, Anouk, and I'm glad to know and work with you.

Introduction

At its most basic, engaging in self-care is about self-respect. Self-care is all about taking care of yourself, making that stand and declaring that, yes, you are important, you do matter. Simple self-care is part of your efforts to be the best person you can be—an idea that resonates in magic as well. Magic is an ideal partner for self-care: one of magic's main focuses is healing—healing of the self, healing of the earth, healing of humanity and nature. In this sense, magic and self-care go hand in hand.

The Witch's Book of Self-Care helps you explore ways to reconnect with yourself, make time for yourself, learn how to experience moments in your day mindfully, and to honor yourself and your spiritual and emotional health. Through magical self-care you will call upon the energies of natural objects such as herbs, stones, and the elements to care for yourself spiritually. Inside these pages you'll discover activities on finding balance, recharging, examining self-destructive behavior and transforming it into a healthier behavior, as well as meditations designed to help you get in touch with yourself again, spiritually and otherwise.

Taking care of your energy, your emotional health, your physical health, and your mental health are all essential undertakings—and can all be enhanced with magic. Being your best self is part of what makes the world a better place. This book can be that first step toward exploring how magic and self-care can partner to support you in your efforts to become the best version of yourself that you can be.

Chapter 1

Self-Care and Magic

Self-care is a buzzword these days. But like media representations of magic, representations of self-care can be confusing. What exactly constitutes self-care? Is getting a mani-pedi or a new handbag actually self-care, and if not, what is? Simply put, self-care is any activity that you do deliberately to take care of your mental, emotional, or physical health.

Magic dovetails perfectly with the concept of self-care because magic is about listening to what's inside you and the messages the Divine and nature have for you. Being in the moment in this way opens you up to an intimate world of information that is supportive of your well-being. Magic and self-care make excellent partners on the road to leading a balanced, fulfilling life.

This chapter will explore not only what self-care is and some of the damaging self-care stereotypes, it will also give you some background on the magical techniques that you will use and explore in the later chapters of this book.

The Goals of Self-Care

The goals of self-care are simple:

- Healthy mind
- Healthy body
- Healthy spirit

The point of self-care isn't just about giving yourself a break. It's about becoming skilled at identifying your needs by listening to your mind, body, and spirit. And not just long-term needs, but also immediate needs, the needs you have at this very moment.

How hard can it be to listen to yourself? Particularly difficult, apparently, because a staggering percentage of the population has difficulty sleeping, anxiety issues, depression, and an ongoing feeling of failure.

Taking care of yourself is more than inputting food and making sure you have a roof over your head. It means treating yourself with the kindness you extend to everyone around you. It means supporting yourself the way you support people who are dear to you.

Women in particular struggle with this self-care issue, although it's not a woman-exclusive problem. Women are socialized to care for the people around them by denying or minimizing their own needs. This leads to an erasure of self-worth and a constant putting-off of rejuvenation or addressing the woman's own needs for support and nurturing. This in turn can lead to anger and resentment.

Self-care means considering yourself a worthwhile person and presenting yourself as valuable, capable, and deserving. In other words, self-care seeks to redress an imbalance that develops when you don't take proper care of yourself, whether by inattention or by choice.

Self-care also doesn't have to involve big, splashy undertakings. In fact, self-care works better if you do it in regular small doses, because it helps keep you from reaching a level where you are in desperate need of something big to make an impact on how you feel. This sort of incremental self-care is also beneficial because small gestures don't take a lot of time, so there is less of a sense of stealing time from other responsibilities or other people. It can help avoid the sense of selfishness that sometimes accompanies self-care activities.

> Often selfishness is at the root of self-care stereotypes. Magical work is excellently poised to fight this feeling, because it generally works on an unseen, inner level where others cannot judge.

Magic As Self-Care

One of magic's main focuses is healing—healing of the self, healing of the earth, healing of humanity and nature. In this sense, magic and self-care go hand in hand. Self-care is a way to maintain your health, heal your spirit, and maintain or optimize your emotional, mental, and physical health. Magic helps with self-empowerment and exerting control over your life, encouraging a focus on yourself as the best person you can be. These are all things that resonate well with the general goal of self-care.

> The practice of magic seeks to establish or balance connection between an individual and the environment. If a spiritual aspect is added, then magic also seeks to balance or maintain the connection between the individual and the Divine.

Incremental Self-Care

There's a tendency for people to say, "Oh, just exercise; your depression will vanish" or "Take up yoga and you'll be a much better person spiritually!"

That's not how self-care works. Self-care is a complicated interwoven combination of hundreds of small acts and an attitude shift. Using just one of the rituals, spells, or practices in this book is not going to solve your problems. But each will make you feel a little better and hopefully help you see that you are worthy of self-care and deserve to take the time and attention you need. Even though it may not make your fatigue vanish completely, taking care of yourself is still a valuable thing. Cleaning up a room won't eliminate your anxiety, but it will make the atmosphere healthier and more comfortable to be in, and that's important.

Fighting the Stereotypes of Self-Care

The media pushes self-care "solutions" in the form of spa days and retail therapy. It's frustrating, because these solutions assume that you are of a certain class with certain options available to you. They assume that you have disposable income; they assume that you actively desire these things and deny yourself for some reason; and they assume that you have the time to engage in these activities, even as a treat.

These media suggestions also assume that engaging in these kinds of activities will fill a gap in your life, implying that you are somehow not normal if engaging in one doesn't fill the void in your heart. Take courage! The media view of self-care does not have to align with your sense of self-care…and, in fact, it's probably healthier if it doesn't.

Self-Care Guilt

Another stereotype of self-care is of someone lazily lounging on a sofa eating chocolate and ignoring chores. This stereotype is harmful in that it suggests taking a few minutes to yourself between tasks is letting an unspecified "everyone" down in some way. It implies that if you're not wholly immersed in handling things, you are failing somehow. This is one of the most harmful stereotypes associated with self-care, because you are being told that you aren't taking things seriously enough if you aren't always working for the benefit of someone other than yourself. It tells you that if you take a moment or two for yourself, you should feel guilty.

While it can be therapeutic to put something off, procrastination or ignoring a problem isn't self-care; in fact, it's the opposite. Ignoring a problem just makes it more of a problem. Self-care involves scheduling things so that they don't reach problem status and includes being kind to your future self by not leaving her a mess to handle.

Releasing Guilt

So often we carry around our guilt and let it fester within us. This is not healthy! Releasing guilt can be very helpful in learning to prioritize self-care. Use the following ritual to let go of some of your guilt and allow yourself to feel the burden of it lifting away from you.

Ritual to Release Guilt

This is a burning ritual in which you burn the thing you are trying to banish or release. This type of ritual can be very therapeutic when you are trying to process painful memories or work through heavy emotions. You may have to do this ritual semiregularly if you tend to feel guilty about different things, or if your guilt about a specific thing pops up again and again. Do it as often as you feel you need to.

This ritual calls for grounding, centering, and optionally casting a circle; if you're not already familiar with these techniques, see the instructions later in this chapter.

What You Need:

- Trivet or hot pad
- Fireproof/heatproof container
- Frankincense incense and a censer
- White candle and candleholder
- Matches or lighter
- Paper
- Pen or pencil

What to Do:

1. Center and ground. Cast a circle if you feel you need one.
2. Place the trivet or hot pad and the heatproof container on top of it next to the incense and candle.
3. Light the frankincense incense. Light the candle.
4. Sit with your eyes closed and think about your sense of guilt. What is it related to? What triggers it? Can you pinpoint what you feel guilty for? There may be associated feelings, such as resentment, sadness, shame, or anger.
5. When you're ready, write these things on the paper.

6. Fold the paper in half or quarters to fit the heatproof container. Hold the paper and say:

   I release this guilt to the universe.
   I invite peace and serenity to take its place.
   Open my heart to the positive energy of this lesson
   And support me as I learn to care for myself freely.
   Thank you for your many blessings.

7. Touch the corner of the paper to the flame of the candle. When the paper catches, place it in the heatproof container and allow it to burn to ash. Allow the incense and candle to burn out.

8. Later, take the ash of the paper and either dispose of it under running water outdoors, or allow the wind to take it.

Hygge and Self-Care

Hygge is a Danish concept that underlines the importance of focusing on the enjoyment of the moment. It's about being present and allowing yourself the time and space to acknowledge a feeling or what's happening at the present moment.

Hygge came about as a result of Danes needing a way to cope emotionally and spiritually with long, cold, dark winters. It celebrates small things that make life worthwhile, such as cups of tea, good books, comfortable spaces, the feeling of security and coziness, home-cooked food, and the company of friends. It rests on the idea of a slow-moving, low-stress, low-commercial-consumption life.

Hygge is a concept that fits almost seamlessly into magical practice. The practice of magic strives for the same sort of serenity that hygge does. Meditation and slowing down to be in the moment, aware and acknowledging your authentic self, is very much at the heart of magic work. Magic looks to improve yourself, to strengthen yourself, and to celebrate yourself.

Hygge suggests that the living of your life can be an art form, which is an excellent way to look at self-care. It's not about flashiness; it's about comfort and expression. It's about creating a special moment, not special in the out-of-the-ordinary sense, but in the recognition that if you pause and allow yourself to acknowledge and connect with that moment, however small, you will realize that every moment can be special just because it's yours and you've recognized it as such.

Part of self-care is allowing yourself the permission to have those moments and to enjoy them. You are encouraged to pause and acknowledge the moment, whether it is good or bad. That moment of acknowledgment reinforces the idea that you are worth the time. It also validates your feelings, which can reduce overall stress. Rather than ignoring your feelings in a mad dash to drive forward, those moments of acknowledging yourself without judgment provide a healthy way to reassure your subconscious that it is allowed to have moods. It doesn't have to be "up" or "on" all the time. In fact, it shouldn't be. Everyone and everything needs downtime.

The Importance of Being Authentic

At its heart, the idea of being authentic means:

- Figuring out who you are
- Accepting yourself
- Being true to yourself

Sound easy? Maybe not.

Often the hustle and bustle of daily life is a way to keep ourselves distracted and busy so that we don't pause and look at ourselves and see who we really are. Pausing to take a good look at yourself can be intimidating. What if you aren't the great person you think you are?

Sometimes self-care is hard because it means facing things you'd rather pretend aren't there. Self-examination is uncomfortable. It requires a level of honesty that you may not feel prepared to handle. You may fear admitting that you have been the one sabotaging yourself, knowingly or unknowingly, or you may be terrified of acknowledging that you need to crack down on your self-discipline in order to be your best self. Self-care means recognizing that you're weak in some areas. It means you have more agency and control over your life than you may be comfortable accepting.

But just think: if you admit you have weak areas, you know what to work on, and you know what parts of you need more love and nurturing. If you accept responsibility for being your best self, then you can make better decisions regarding your self-care.

Try this affirmation: "*I honor my true self.*"

Living as your authentic self means following a very individual path. No one else can live quite like you. It's a unique pursuit. Yes, it is hard to isolate your own values and sometimes harder to live according to them when it might be a lot easier to remain ignorant and pretend that you're fine. But caring for an inauthentic self is like filling a leaky bucket. You can't ever fill it, because it's not complete. Self-care means valuing all the various parts of you, not just some of them (yes, even the parts that still need work). If you pretend to be someone you're not, how can you ever be truly happy? If you're not being authentic, how can you have compassion for yourself?

Living authentically might not be easy, but it's rewarding. Here are some things to keep in mind:

- Balance what you feel and/or need against your actions.
- Making value-based choices will be healthier in the long run than making choices based on convenience or popular opinion.
- Advocate for yourself and your needs or wants.
- Don't let yourself be driven by a need to be approved of or liked by others. Approval is a powerful drug, but being happy with your value-based choices is healthier for your spirit and sense of self.

Being openly authentic can be intimidating. What if you embrace yourself as you truly are, weaknesses and flaws and all…only to be rejected by other people? Fear is a powerful deterrent. Fear of failure, of rejection, or of loneliness can combine with the fear of missing out, creating a tangle of anxiety and a sense of not being in control of anything. Remember, though, living authentically will build your sense of confidence and strength, which will in turn show in your personal energy.

Author Brené Brown talks about cultivating the ability to be imperfect in *The Gifts of Imperfection*. Accepting that you are imperfect and still worth caring for is a valuable practice in your self-care toolbox.

As much as self-examination can be scary, ignoring it just creates a different kind of stress—avoidable stress, at that. Make the choice to work through the stress and engage in self-reflection instead of being at the mercy of the stress that rises from procrastinating or ignoring something. Be in control. (Check out the exercise Authenticity: A Spell to Help Recognize the Real You, in Chapter 2.)

Magical Techniques for Self-Care

This book proposes a variety of magical techniques to use in your practice of self-care. Most of them are easy and accessible, and others ask for minor purchases of herbs or stones. Stones don't need to be huge; even a small stone possesses natural energy that you can draw on to help support your own. Most of the herbs can be found in a grocery store. Some can be used in oil form. Essential oils may seem expensive, but they are concentrated and last a long time with proper storage away from light. Here are some of the magical techniques you will explore throughout this book.

Creative Visualization

Were you called out for daydreaming or having an overactive imagination as a child? Creative visualization is a technique that uses your powers of imagination and concentration to create an image of the reality you're working for. It's more focused than daydreaming and requires you to create what you're visualizing with care. Essentially, by visualizing a potential situation and lending it energy, you're fueling it and giving it more power.

Creative visualization also works in a negative way. This is why you need to catch yourself in the act if your mind goes off on a tangent imagining something terrible. You don't want to give a negative outcome any more power or fuel than it already possesses.

Meditation

Meditation offers your mind a break by allowing it to disengage from the ongoing commotion of the world around you. It has physical benefits, such as slowing heart rate and lowering blood pressure. Mentally, it improves concentration and counters stress, depression, and anxiety, as well as fighting recursive negative thinking. Emotionally, meditation encourages self-acceptance and optimism. Spiritually, it fosters calm, serenity, and a sense of peace and harmony with the universe.

The types of meditation explored in this book include mindfulness meditation and breathing meditation, both very simple practices that encourage self-care.

Breathing Exercises

Breathing exercises allow you to pay attention to what is otherwise an autonomous function. For an autonomous function, it's impressive how much improvement you can realize with a bit of attention to the process!

By taking control of your breathing, you can affect the depth and rhythm of your intake and release of oxygen. In turn, that can benefit your brain function, your heart rate, the health of your body in general, and more. Breathing exercises can also do double duty as meditation.

Herbal Magic

What's the difference between herbal magic and herbalism? Herbalism works on a medicinal level. Magic works with the energies of the plant. The two are not mutually exclusive. For example, there are tea recipes in this book that incorporate both herbal magic and medicinal herbalism. Mainly, however, the energies of flowers, shrubs, herbs, and trees are used to support and encourage self-care magically as opposed to medicinally for the physical body.

Herbal magic can be used in aromatherapy, incense, oils, potpourri, sachets, powders, charms, and as a supportive magical technique for other kinds of magic.

Candle Magic

Apart from candles providing an excellent way to create a welcoming atmosphere, candle magic is simple and serene. It can be as simple as lighting a candle and enjoying the beauty of the flame and the scent, or it can be more complicated, involving carving words into the candle or drilling holes in the wax, which you then fill with herbs and/or oils. Candles provide an easy way to engage in self-care; you don't need to invest in expensive ones, although seeking out the cheapest options often means you might end up with poorly made candles that burn unevenly, smoke, and leave messy black soot on the walls.

You can also purchase your own ingredients and supplies and enjoy rolling, dipping, or pouring your own candles, which allows you to add powdered dried herbs and oils to the candles as they are being made.

Here are some tips for candles:

- Buy a box of any size of Mason jars (or grab them when you see them at thrift stores) and use them as candleholders, either for tea lights or pillars. Tie a bit of ribbon or raffia around each jar for rustic charm. (Make sure the ribbon or raffia isn't too close to the top of the jar so it's safe from the flame.) Swap the colors of ribbons or raffia as the seasons change, if you like.

- Grease the inside of the bottom of the jar with petroleum jelly or olive oil to help prevent the candle from sticking to the bottom once it has finished burning.

- Always use a proper candle snuffer to put out the flame instead of trying to blow the flame out to avoid spattering wax.

- Look for soy candles or ones with a high percentage of beeswax. Not only do they burn more cleanly, they also release fewer harmful chemicals into the air and are likely to be made under better working conditions.

- Practice sensible fire safety around candles. Don't leave them unattended, and make sure there is nothing flammable around them.

Crystal and Gem Magic

Like candles, crystals and other stones can be a passive part of your self-care, or they can take a more active part if you charge or program them to direct their energies toward a specific purpose. Crystals and stones are terrific little batteries with native energy that you can access easily. They're generally small enough to slip into a pocket or bag, or you can find jewelry set with stones that align with your desired goal. Stones are reusable, too; give them a good cleansing (see the instructions for cleansing/purifying later in this chapter), and they're good to go again.

Magical Basics

The main focus of this book is not to teach the basics of magical practice. However, in the interest of giving everyone a level playing field, what follows are some bare-bones foundational techniques that will be called on in this book.

> For a more in-depth look at magical techniques, please see my books *Power Spellcraft for Life* and *Solitary Wicca for Life*.

Center and Ground

This is an essential magical technique that ties especially well into self-care. It's a practice that can calm agitated personal energy, replenish low personal energy, and create a sense of belonging, connection, and reassurance.

Center and Ground

This is the first thing you should do before engaging in any kind of magical work, to ensure that you don't drain your personal energy during the working.

What to Do:

1. Close your eyes and take three slow breaths.
2. Visualize a light in the core of your body. What you consider your body's core is up to you; some people locate it around the heart, others, the solar plexus or lower in the abdomen. What's important is that it makes sense to you as the location of your core.
3. Visualize a tendril of light growing down from your core toward the ground. See it reach down through the surface, deep into the earth's core. Visualize your tendril of energy meeting the energy of the earth. Draw some of the earth's energy up that tendril as if it were a straw, bringing it up into your body. Let the energy of the earth fill you.
4. If you are tired or low on energy, you can use this earth energy to replenish or rebalance yourself.
5. If you are jumpy or buzzing with extra energy that's making you jittery or flighty, then once you have connected your energy to that of the earth, visualize some of your personal energy bleeding off to be absorbed by the earth.

This process can be easier to visualize if you imagine the energy of the earth to be a different color from your personal energy.

Circles

A magic circle is an energy barrier created to delineate a sacred space in which to worship, a container created to protect what is inside or to keep unwanted energy out, and provides a way to collect focused energy while it is raised before that energy is released toward a goal. You might not always need a circle, but how to cast one is a good technique to know because the circle can also function as a personal shield to ward off negative energy.

Casting a Circle

Here is how to cast and take down a magic circle.

What to Do:

1. Center and ground.
2. Draw energy up from the earth into your core and let it flow down the arm of your dominant hand.
3. Imagine the earth energy flowing out of your fingers. Point your hand to the side and either turn slowly in place or walk around the perimeter of your space, visualizing the energy flowing out like a ribbon to surround your working area. Finish the circle by visualizing the ribbon of energy meeting the other end you started with.
4. Once the ring of energy is complete, visualize the energy stretching up to form walls, then continuing into a dome over your head. Visualize a similar hemisphere under you, so that the energy surrounds you like a full sphere.
5. When your work is complete, visualize this in reverse. See the half spheres above and below you recede back into the simple ribbon

of energy circled around you. Then point your hand at where the circle began and ended and trace it in reverse, imagining the energy flowing back to your hand and up your arm to your core. Make sure to allow it to flow past your core and down your connection to the earth to allow it to rejoin the earth energy it came from.

Sacred Space

Sacred space is space devoted to your best self. A magical circle created to set apart a bit of the everyday world is one form of temporary sacred space, but sacred space can also be made with intention in other ways. This is probably the technique that you will use most often in pursuit of self-care.

Methods of creating sacred space can include:

- Lighting a candle and incense dedicated to that purpose.
- Sprinkling blessed water (made by adding a pinch of salt to a cup of water) around an area.
- Strewing herbs.
- Blessing an area with all four elements (earth, air, fire, and water). A simple way to do this is to use incense, which represents fire and air, and blessed water, which represents earth and water.

Cleansing/Purifying Objects

Before you use items in magic, it's always a good idea to cleanse their energy. Energy tends to collect on objects, especially objects that are handled by people. You may have programmed some items to do specific energy work, like absorb negativity or protect or draw something toward yourself. At the end of their purpose, it's a good idea to run them through a magical wash to get it clean for the next time you need it.

> Don't worry; cleansing something won't remove an item's innate energy. In other words, you don't need to worry about wiping away clear quartz's ability to supply you with energy or obsidian's ability to protect you from negativity.

Here are a few different ways to cleanse something magically:

- Place the item in sunlight or moonlight for about 24 hours. Put a small mirror underneath it to increase the efficiency of the purification.
- Place the item in a container of salt. Warning: don't do this with metal items, as they can corrode. This works best with stones and crystals.
- Place the item in a dish of sand or earth and cover it lightly. Wrap the item in a light cloth first, if you like.
- Pass the item through smoke of sandalwood, frankincense, or myrrh incense. (See Chapter 5 for incense recipes.)
- Hold the item in your hands, or hold your hands above it with the palms down. Center and ground, then draw up energy from the earth. Imagine it flowing down to your hands and surrounding the object. Say, *"With this energy I cleanse you; with this energy you are cleared of all external energy. May it be so."*

Mindfulness

Mindfulness is not a technique so much as an important aspect of magical practice. Mindfulness is being in the moment, allowing whatever task you're performing to have the whole of your attention in a relaxed fashion, so that you are fully open to the experience.

Mindfulness is important in magic because you are tied to your environment, which impacts you. Being aware of everything is critical to being able to pick and choose what you want to draw on in your magical work. It's also important because you need to be able to differentiate between good and bad (or supportive and unsupportive) energy.

Reaching out and being able to sense what is around you takes a curious blend of concentration and release. Check out the awareness and sensory exercises in Chapter 2 to work on practicing mindfulness.

Magical Journaling for Self-Care

Journaling is a therapeutic practice. It's also a valuable part of working magic. Keeping records of your work allows you to consult notes regarding herbal or incense blends, timing, successes and failures, origins of ideas, references, and experiments with energies of various supplies and components. Partnering or uniting the concepts of reflective self-care journaling and magical journaling in pursuit of self-care just makes sense.

You'll have more than one magical and/or self-care journal in your life, so don't get too caught up in finding the perfect one to last forever. Any blank journal or notebook that is pretty and makes you happy or relaxed when looking at it is great.

Do you already keep a magical journal, recording your energy work, spells, and rituals? Decide if you want to have a separate self-care journal or if you're going to use your existing magical journal for that purpose. Do what feels right for you. You can always start one way and switch later if your initial choice doesn't work for you.

A self-care journal tip: glue an envelope to the back cover, or use washi tape to tape the bottom and side of the last two pages to make a pocket open at the top. This allows you to keep loose things in it.

The following rituals will help get you started with your journaling practice. The first is a simple technique to bless your new self-care journal. The second establishes optimal conditions to allow a productive journaling session.

Self-Care Journal Dedication

Before you start using new tools, it's a good idea to cleanse and bless them or dedicate them to their intended purpose. This ritual calls for a candle and incense that will be used for your future self-care journaling sessions as well as this initial blessing. Why not start using a new pen as well? Keep it just for use with your self-care journal.

What You Need:

* Candle in a color you associate with clarity and self-reflection (some suggestions: white, pale blue, pale yellow) and a candleholder
* Incense of your choice (suggestions: sandalwood, frankincense, lavender, jasmine) and a censer
* Matches or lighter
* New notebook
* Pen
* Markers, stickers, washi tape, and so on (optional; see instructions)

What to Do:

1. Center and ground.
2. Light the candle and the incense. Sit or stand in a relaxed way, eyes closed, and let yourself be in the moment for a minute or so.
3. Pick up the notebook and pass it over the candle, then through the incense, saying, "*I cleanse you of negative energy.*" Repeat with the pen.
4. Hold the book and close your eyes. Take a few slow breaths. Say:

    > *May this book encourage me to value myself,*
    > *To care for myself as I deserve,*
    > *And to celebrate myself.*
    > *It is my friend and my support. May it be so!*

5. Write this (or a blessing of your own creation) on the first page of the journal. Decorate it as you like with markers, stickers, washi tape...whatever makes you feel warm and happy when you look at it.

Tips:

◆ You can use a series of small candles or you can dedicate a large pillar candle to your journaling sessions. If you do the latter, you can pierce holes in the top of the candle and carefully drip essential oil into them or load it with powdered herbs to add their energies to the experience. (See the Enhancing Home Energy Pillar Candle project in Chapter 5.)

◆ If you're using stick incense, you don't have to let a whole stick burn every time you light it. If you're finished before the incense stick is, just tamp it out gently in the censer and slip it back in the packet for next time. Or break one in half and use only one half at a time. Experiment and see what works for you.

Journaling Framework Ritual

Using magical ritual is a way of setting an action or sequence apart from the everyday world. Repeating a certain sequence of actions also allows you to become very familiar with what comes next in the sequence. In the case of this framework, it trains your mind to quickly slip into the calm headspace that is ideal for reflective journaling.

This framework is designed to allow you to slip into the optimal frame of mind for the several journaling exercises throughout the book. Why not brew a cup of tea to go along with it, or pour yourself something refreshing?

This framework calls for a candle and incense of your choice, preferably in colors and scents you associate with peace and clarity. Use the same candle and incense for your self-care journaling session each time. The familiar setting will act as a trigger to help you reach a relaxed, self-reflective state more easily every time. You could use a meditation incense here as well (see Chapter 5).

What You Need:

* Your journaling candle in a candleholder (see earlier in this chapter)
* Your journaling incense and a censer (see earlier in this chapter)
* Matches or lighter
* Your magical self-care journal and pen (see earlier in this chapter)

What to Do:

1. Center and ground.

2. Light the candle and incense, saying, *"Peace surround me; I am present in the moment."*

3. Sit in a relaxed way, eyes closed, and let yourself be in the moment for a minute or so. Then open your eyes, open your notebook, and journal whatever you intend to record.

4. When you are done, close the book and say, *"I thank the universe for my many opportunities to reflect and explore my spirit. May I always be blessed."*

Tip:

+ Try playing the same album or playlist of relaxed, meditative music while you journal, to further create the self-care atmosphere.

Chapter 2

Mental and Emotional Self-Care

This chapter focuses on the general self-care of your personal energy to help stay in good shape mentally and emotionally. It looks at attitudes, relationships, and how to maintain a broad balance in all the areas of your life. Each of these spheres (and the physical and spiritual areas of your life as well; see Chapters 3 and 4) can and do influence one another. If you work on improving self-care in one area, that will automatically support other spheres as well. Self-care has a cascading benefit.

Identifying Your Self-Care Goals

How do you begin your self-care? First think: What do you live for? What is your bliss? What makes you feel good?

Being able to pin this down is valuable, because without goals you can end up flailing around, trying to make yourself feel better in general, without addressing the source(s) of your imbalances. Identifying your self-care goals means a more efficient and effective application of your time and energy into your self-care. Knowing these goals informs the quality of your self-care and also facilitates your commitment to living authentically.

Making a Self-Care Vision Board (see the following) is one way to work through the process of identifying your self-care goals.

Self-Care Vision Board

A vision board is a themed collection of images, quotations, and objects mounted on a flat surface. When you create a vision board and place it in a space where you see it often, you essentially end up doing short visualization exercises throughout the day every time you see it. Consciously or unconsciously, seeing it sends cues to your spirit and reactivates the energy you have tied into those goals. Visualization is a powerful tool in self-care.

When designing a vision board, the focus should be on how you want things to be. Choose things to include that elicit the emotions you want to feel, that remind you of the life you want to have. Focus more on the less-tangible aspects of the life you want to have; it's nice to wish for material things, but that's not what this is really about. Your vision board should motivate and inspire you to work toward the quality of life you want to be living.

Creating your vision board is going to be a unique and personal process. What you use as a foundation for your board will depend on your budget, the space you have to display it, and your creative choices. You could use a corkboard or poster board from a craft store or repurpose a frame that you already have by replacing the contents with blank card stock. You could even cut a piece of poster board into a specific shape.

Spend some time ahead of this activity to think about what kind of themes you want to represent. You might want to spend time searching for specific images or artwork. Also give some thought to whether you want this board to be permanent or an ongoing evolution that reflects how your needs for self-care change.

You might want to make a new one annually and keep past ones to look back on, or you might decide that the evolution itself is what's important.

What You Need:

- A foundation for your board (corkboard, poster board, and so on)
- Blank card stock
- Pens or markers
- Photos, souvenirs, and trinkets that support or evoke your goals
- Glue, tape, or pushpins (depending on your foundation board)
- Washi tape, stickers, and so on (optional; see instructions)

What to Do:

1. Gather your supplies.
2. If you like, use the Journaling Framework Ritual in Chapter 1 to prepare for the activity, including the candle and incense, if you use them. Otherwise, create a pleasant ambience to work in: adjust the lighting, put on relaxing or motivational music, and so forth.
3. Design your board. Do you want space between the objects on your board or do you want them to overlap? Also decide if you want to fill the board completely or leave space for new things as they come into importance in your life.
4. Write an affirmation or a short list of self-care goals on the piece of card stock and position it on the board.
5. Arrange the items around the affirmation or list as you like without attaching them. When you have decided on your layout, fasten your items to the board with pins, glue, or tape. Use the washi tape and stickers, if you like, to further decorate the vision board.
6. Display the Self-Care Vision Board in your chosen location.

Affirmations

Positive thinking has gotten a lot of flak from the mainstream media and pundits for being a fluffy way to try to effect change. At the same time, however, studies in psychology analyze how hearing negative talk over and over can damage the development of the young psyche. Negative self-talk can do similar damage. Thought patterns can impact your health. Rewiring your brain by repeating something is easy to do…it just happens most often that you do it unintentionally and in a negative fashion. The mind is a powerful thing, and it is very open to suggestion.

Here's the thing: you are the person who speaks to yourself most often. You hear yourself speak more than anyone else in the world. So be kind to yourself.

Our self-talk is often punishingly hard. It's aggressive, condescending, bullying, abusive, and downright mean. If someone spoke that way to another person, you'd be shocked, horrified, perhaps moved to intervene. So why don't we recognize it in ourselves?

Well, for one thing, it's all internal, and most of the time we don't notice.

It can be very difficult to retrain your inner voice to be nurturing. Sometimes thinking of yourself as a child can help. *"Did that hurt?"* you can ask yourself. *"It looks like it did. It's okay. It hurts, but it will be over soon. Hey, look at that pretty butterfly. I wonder where it's going right now?"* Just as you'd affirm a child's emotion and then help redirect their attention from the subject that's upsetting them, you can redirect your own focus too. There are lots of exercises about mindfulness in this book; working on being in the moment and letting thoughts flow past you without getting caught up in them is training that helps immensely with handling negative self-talk.

Affirmations are another handy, easy way to address negative self-talk. An affirmation is a positive statement that reinforces a desired goal or circumstance or that counters something negative. If you catch yourself criticizing something you said or did, a decision you made, or something you failed to do, take a moment to clear your mind, take a couple of slow breaths, and repeat an affirmation like one of these simple, one-sentence affirmations:

- *I am allowed to make mistakes.*
- *I made a decision, one among many. It is past.*
- *I will do better next time.*
- *I am right where I need to be.*
- *I am enough.*
- *I have the power to change myself and my world.*

Is saying a simple sentence going to change things just like that? Alas, it's not that easy. It's the repetition that's key. By repeating positive affirmations like these and others, you can start to rewire your brain to be more positive, optimistic, and confident.

If you learn well by writing things out, write out your affirmation(s) in your self-care journal. Don't use too many at once; work on two or three at a time, maximum, then move on to another set after a month or two.

Starting Your Day with Self-Care

Carving out a quiet space for yourself before your day begins in earnest is a valuable practice that helps you slip into a grounded headspace from which to approach your routine. If this routine doesn't work for you, tweak it until it addresses your needs.

Daily 5-Minute Self-Care Routine to Start the Day

This is a regular self-care version of this routine. For a specific spiritual version, see the Daily Kickoff Ritual in Chapter 4. You could also pair the two for the best possible way to start your day.

What to Do:

1. Wake up. Stretch. Suggested yoga poses you can do without leaving your bed: Child, Cobra, Cat/Cow, Pigeon.
2. Sit cross-legged and close your eyes. Breathe deeply and run your awareness over your body. Is there anywhere that hurts, that feels off, that might need extra attention today?
3. Get up. Drink a glass of water with awareness. Notice the sensation of the liquid in your mouth, the muscles moving as you swallow.
4. Mentally review your schedule for the day, perhaps while you have your first cup of tea or coffee. Take a moment to open your mind and accept your upcoming tasks. Don't go into detail about how you'll execute them; just accept that they're on the list of things to do.

5. Choose an affirmation for your day based on your physical body scan, your upcoming schedule for the day, and your general mood. Affirmations like *"I am enough,"* *"I meet challenges with grace,"* and *"I am calm and capable"* are good all-purpose statements, but it's preferable to tailor your affirmation to your needs.

6. And...go!

Tip:

♦ An additional 5 minutes to work with your self-care journal can be a beneficial complement to this basic morning self-care list. (You could write out your chosen daily affirmation a few times to help it sink in!) See the Daily Kickoff Ritual in Chapter 4 for more ideas.

Authenticity

Self-care can be tough. You need to see who you truly are in order to take care of yourself properly. Defining the different parts of yourself is a great exercise in self-acceptance. The following spell will help you discover and acknowledge all the different parts of who you are, and the affirmations that follow will help you keep in mind how great that person is.

Authenticity: A Spell to Help Recognize the Real You

Here's a spell to help with insight into who you are, so that you can more easily embrace yourself.

What You Need:

• Paper
• Pencil or pen (or colored pencils/markers; see instructions)

What to Do:

1. Center and ground. Take a few deep, slow breaths.
2. Write your name in the center of the paper.
3. Start writing words around your name that reflect who you are—not who you *wish* you were; who you *truly are* on the inside. Shy? Scared? Melancholy? Geek? Scared of rejection? Feel left behind by friends you knew in college? Worried your supervisor doesn't understand your approach? Enthusiastic fan of various film franchises? Write it down. No one is going to see this but you. Be precise. Don't judge. Don't make excuses. But don't leave out the good stuff. Do you make a terrific cheesecake? Are you a sympathetic listener? Do you have an excellent sense of humor? Are you a runner, a knitter, a gamer?

4. Hold the paper and say:

    Inside,
    Past the outside,
    No more hiding.
    I am myself,
    I am enough,
    I am worth love.

5. Fold up the paper and slip it into your self-care journal. Review
    it every once in a while when you feel like you're losing the sense
    of yourself.

Tip:

♦   Write a new authenticity spell a few times a year, if you feel the
    desire to. Make sure to date each one so you can properly trace the
    evolution when you review them. You should see core concepts pop
    up again and again. Those describe you at your center.

Authenticity Affirmations

Staying authentic to who you are at heart and in your spirit will be an
ongoing challenge. When you feel like you're slipping into pretending
to be someone else, or when you're making choices because they seem
easy instead of right (we all do it sometimes, but when it becomes habit
because it's simpler than the alternative, that's when it's time to revisit
the previous Authenticity spell), working with authenticity-themed
affirmations can help you remember to stay on track.

Perhaps you're nervous about making the changes that family, friends, or colleagues may question or challenge. Reinforce your
commitment to being authentic by using these affirmations to remind
yourself that you have the right to be who your spirit tells you to be.

What to Do:

These single-sentence affirmations can be written down, spoken aloud as part of meditation, repeated in your heart or aloud while looking yourself in the eye in the mirror, written on sticky notes and posted around your cubicle, typed out in a beautiful font and used as the lock screen on your phone, and more. The possibilities are limitless.

+ *I am valid.*
+ *I am the person I wish to be.*
+ *I am the best version of myself that I can be.*
+ *I release all false projections of myself and embrace my true spirit.*
+ *I am vibrant and creative.*
+ *My actions and choices reflect my values.*
+ *I am at home in my heart and spirit.*
+ *I honor who I am.*

Tips:

+ Want to use all these statements as part of a litany? Go for it!
+ As always, tweak these affirmations if you feel the desire to, and write your own to tailor them exactly to your needs.

Journaling Exercises

A great way to remember that happiness is within reach is to list things that bring you joy; write them in your self-care journal. This can sometimes be overwhelming or daunting to do without a context, so a great way to approach it is to work with a specific subject. The following journaling exercises will help you explore some specific details to give you insight into your larger self.

Journaling Exercise: Sensory Gratitude

One way to feel more connected to the world around you—and to discover how you can further expand your methods of self-care—is to explore your relationship with your physical senses. What brings you joy when using your senses?

What You Need:
* Self-care journal
* Pen or pencil

What to Do:
1. Center and ground.
2. Take a few moments to open your mind and think about each sense in turn. Write down your answers, then move on to thinking about the next sense.

    * What sights bring you joy?
    * What sounds bring you joy?
    * What scents bring you joy?
    * What tastes bring you joy?
    * What brings you joy when you touch it?

3. Don't censor or criticize yourself as you make your lists. No one is going to see this other than yourself. If you like burying your face in kitten fur, write it down. If you like the smell of a freshly uncapped marker or a just-extinguished match, write it down.

4. The lists don't need to be exhaustive. It's enough to list one or two things during this round.

This journaling exercise makes you think about your relationship with your senses in a nonabstract way. It also helps you think about specific moments within larger actions. The smell of a freshly extinguished match is a very specific moment in the larger process of striking the match, lighting something with the flame, and then shaking or tamping out the match. Now that you know the specific moment is something that brings you joy, you can take pleasure in it the next time you light and extinguish a match. To fully recognize and appreciate it as an enjoyable sensation, be fully present in the moment that it happens.

Journaling Exercise: Seasonal Gratitude

Journaling gratitude can help you recognize more opportunities to practice thankfulness. As with joy, journaling a broad topic like gratitude can sometimes be overwhelming or daunting to do without a context, so this exercise offers you the chance to explore gratitude within a seasonal context. See also Chapter 4 for ideas about working with seasonal energies to engage in self-care.

What You Need:
◆ Self-care journal   ◆ Pen or pencil

What to Do:
1. Center and ground.

2. Take a few moments to open your mind and think about each season in turn. Write down your answers, then move on to thinking about the next season.

   • What are you thankful for in the spring?
   • What are you thankful for in the summer?
   • What are you thankful for in the fall?
   • What are you thankful for in the winter?

3. Don't censor or criticize yourself as you make your lists. No one is going to see this other than yourself. If you're thankful for having an excuse to stay inside more during winter, write it down.

4. The lists don't need to be exhaustive. It's enough to list one or two things during this round.

Tip:

• If you live in a geographic location that doesn't have a lot of variation between the seasons, think about the yearly calendar instead. For example, how are the seasons reflected in the produce available to you or the seasonal decorations in your town?

Journaling Exercise: Daily Gratitude

One of the principles in magic is that like attracts like. The idea behind listing things you're grateful for is that it invites you to recognize more blessings or good things for which to be grateful. This exercise is also good for mental and emotional health. When you make a point of listing good things that happened or things you accomplished, then you start to validate your own successes. It's healthy to be proud of getting through the day if it was hard. Go you!

At the end of the day, sit down with your self-care journal and write these things:

1. Three successes. *You* define what success is. If you deal with a chronic illness, a success can be "I got out of bed" or "I ate breakfast." Maybe a success is remembering to take your multivitamin or remembering to hydrate enough to finish two refills of your water bottle at work. The key is that you have to consider it a success within the context of the kind of day you had.

2. Three things that brought you joy. Again, you get to define what a joy was on that particular day. Did your favorite song play on the radio on the way to work? Did this month's issue of your favorite magazine subscription land in your mailbox? Did you see a cute cat on the way home? If it made you happy, write it down.

3. Three things you're thankful for. Were you grateful for catching the early train so you had a bit of extra time to settle in before class started? Was there a computer server issue at work so you got to come home early and sit in the sun with a good book? Were you there when a friend needed to touch base today? Write it down.

Is coming up with three things hard to manage? Start with one thing in each category, then move up to two, and finally to three. You'll find that it gets easier the more you practice it.

After doing this for a few days, you may notice that your mood in general has improved, because you're focusing on positive stuff instead of the bad things that happen to you. The negative things tend to stick with you more easily than the positive ones; when you finally manage to put the bad things out of your mind, something will remind you of them and—guess what?—they're back. Practicing daily gratitude by choosing to record good things instead of bad means that you are consciously choosing to search your memory for positive events. It's another form of rewiring your brain and redirecting your thought patterns. And apart from that, it just makes you feel good to remember the nice stuff that happened.

Spells to Battle Stress

Managing stress and anxiety improves your daily functioning, enabling you to cope more effectively with the very situations that can stress you. Managing stress can improve your physical, mental, and emotional health, as well as support your self-esteem and confidence. See the section on meditation in Chapter 4 for more techniques that can help you cope with stress.

Fill Yourself with Light

Taking a few minutes to fill yourself with light can give you the mental break you need to reset your headspace. It can also function like a quick cleanse of your aura (personal energy that surrounds you). This is an excellent way to take hold of yourself if you are stressed or panicky.

What to Do:

1. Center and ground.
2. Close your eyes and take three slow breaths. With each breath in, imagine yourself drawing in light through your nose or mouth. With each breath, imagine your body filling with light. After your third breath, breathe normally, eyes still closed, enjoying the sensation of being filled with light. Note how it makes you feel emotionally as well as physically.
3. Allow the light to begin to expand past your body into your aura. As it passes into the aura, imagine it beginning to sparkle. Imagine sparkles loosening and clearing away any negativity or unwanted energy clinging to your aura.
4. When you feel that you are done, take one final deep breath and exhale with conviction. Allow the visualization to fade, then open your eyes.

Transformation

Sometimes you can feel stuck in a rut. You know you were headed somewhere, but along the way you either derailed or ran out of steam. The transformation you seek feels stalled. In cases like this, grand gestures can do more to destabilize you than help. Instead, work for patience and clarity to help you refocus, and open yourself to change to help ease the transformation.

What You Need:
- White candle and candleholder
- Matches or lighter
- Clear quartz stone

What to Do:
1. Cleanse the materials according to your chosen method(s) (see Chapter 1).
2. Center and ground. Light the white candle and hold the quartz crystal in your hands. Close your eyes and breathe evenly, bringing your body and spirit to a sense of equilibrium.
3. When you are ready, lift the quartz crystal and hold it to your forehead.
4. Say, "*I call on light to help me see clearly. May I be open to the change working in my life; may I have the patience to allow it the time it needs to develop, to gestate, to unfold, and to weave itself into my life securely. May this change be for the best and benefit me and those I hold dear. It is so.*"

Exercise: Five Things That Stress You

As uncomfortable as it may be, sometimes you need to take time to think about things that trigger anxiety. It is valuable to know what knocks you off balance or what clouds your thought process because the situation is ratcheting up your stress level. Take the time to think about things that stress you, then make this list in a safe place in a calm frame of mind.

What You Need:

- Journaling candle in a candleholder (see Chapter 1)
- Journaling incense (see Chapter 1)
- Self-care journal
- Pen or pencil

What to Do:

1. Center and ground.
2. Light the journaling candle and incense. Open your journal to a new page and mark the date and topic.
3. Take a few moments to settle yourself comfortably. Close your eyes and breathe deeply for a few breaths.
4. In this safe place, think honestly about what situations create stress. Write them down as they come to you. If you prefer, write down your thoughts as they come in a stream-of-consciousness record, then sift out the distilled points at the end of the exercise.
5. Don't make excuses and don't judge as you write. In order for this exercise to be as valuable as possible, you have to be as honest as you can.
6. Don't worry if you can't be very precise about your stressors. The mind spends a lot of time avoiding thinking too hard about danger and things that can trigger stress, since even thinking

about stressors can elicit a response similar to those caused by a real-life stress encounter. Do the best you can in this session.

7. If at any time you find yourself having a stressful reaction beyond what you feel you can handle, allow yourself to end the journaling session. Return to it a day or two later. Don't avoid it for too long; the point of this exercise is to recognize and isolate the situations that stress you so that you can work to head them off or learn to cope better during them.

8. To finish the session, close your journal. Close your eyes and breathe deeply for a few breaths, then open your eyes and extinguish the candle and incense. Alternatively, you may allow both to burn out on their own.

Organization and Planning Help

One of the things that probably stresses you the most is how to break larger tasks down into manageable ones. Here's a list of suggestions:

+ Look at the due date of a task or deadline you are facing. List all the elements of the project that need to be addressed before then.

+ Assign smaller due dates to smaller elements of the project. Start with the parts that later parts will be dependent on.

+ Build wiggle room into your schedule to account for illness or other emergencies you may have to handle.

+ Don't procrastinate. Don't let all the work fall on the shoulders of "Future You." That's an abuse of your own energy and disrespect of your future self.

+ Use alarms, reminders, pretty sticky notes, a calendar grid with different colored markers to note various steps of your process—anything and everything that can help you stay on top of what needs to be done and when.

+ There are also some magical things you can do to lessen the stress of planning and organizing, including making a special charm bag and keeping track of your self-care.

Planning and Organization Charm Bag

You can make a small charm bag or bottle to help you cope with keeping everything organized. Brown jasper, a kind of quartz, helps with long-term energy maintenance; mint helps with focus; and ylang-ylang and bergamot oils help with staying calm while still attentive.

What You Need:

- Small bowl for mixing
- 1 teaspoon dried mint
- 3 drops ylang-ylang essential oil
- 2 drops bergamot essential oil
- Brown jasper stone
- Small bag or sachet (color of your choice) or small glass bottle or jar

What to Do:

1. Start by cleansing/purifying your supplies as per your preferred method (see Chapter 1).
2. Center and ground.
3. Place the mint in the bowl, saying, *"Mint, bring me focus so that I can keep my mind on my tasks."*
4. Add the drops of ylang-ylang essential oil to the mint, saying, *"Ylang-ylang, bring me your peace and serenity so that I remain calm in the face of my schedule."*
5. Add the drops of bergamot essential oil, saying, *"Bergamot, bring me clarity and confidence."*
6. Hold the brown jasper, and say, *"I call on your energies of management and organization. Bring me long-term capability to schedule, plan, and manage my time."* Place it in the bowl.
7. Stir with your fingers, saying, *"I am calm, I am focused, I manage my time confidently. So may it be!"*
8. Pour or scoop the mix into the sachet or jar and tie it closed or put the lid on. Hang or place it next to your wall calendar, or carry it with your agenda or journal.

Tip:

- If you make a miniature version of this, it could be small enough to tie onto your agenda or journal as a charm or hang on your calendar.

Track Your Self-Care

If you struggle with a chronic condition or are overwhelmed by trying to organize your life, start by tracking only three or four of your self-care successes at once. Recognizing a success can give you the sense of accomplishment that helps support a positive mood.

Instead of writing on loose paper, you could use your self-care journal or start a separate small notebook for habit tracking.

What You Need:
* Paper or notebook   * Pen

What to Do:
1. For a simple self-care tracker covering the basics of self-care, draw a chart with a row for each day of the month, and four columns. Label the first column "Hours of Sleep," the second "Ate Properly," the third "Exercised" (if *exercise* is a trigger word for you, label it "Moved" instead), and the fourth "Something Kind I Did for Myself." This covers self-care basics: adequate rest, adequate food and movement, and one act of self-care that doesn't classify as belonging in one of the previous columns.
2. Write the hours of sleep you got in as soon as you wake up. At the end of each day, think back and mark off the other three columns, or mark them off as you accomplish them during the day.
3. The moving/exercise column can cover things like walking to the bus stop or to work from the subway, taking a 5-minute brisk walk at lunch, remembering to sit back and stretch regularly at work, doing the vacuuming, mowing the lawn—anything that gets you moving.
4. Over time, you'll be able to see your patterns of sleep, movement, and self-nourishment. This will allow you to pat yourself on the back for the successes as well as target weak spots to focus on in order to improve your self-care.

Slow Down and Treat Yourself

Treating yourself is a fun way to engage in some self-care. We often think of a treat being food or drink or some sort of retail therapy. But it can be curling up with a book and a cup of tea or sitting in the sun with a cat on your lap.

> Don't multitask by combining your treats, unless you specifically design one as something stacked (a fancy coffee while reading a good book, for example). If you overload your treat time, you'll lose out on the full experience of enjoying each aspect, and the self-care might become perfunctory.

There are a few things to keep in mind about treating yourself. If your treat is commonplace, it won't be a treat. Try to keep it as something special that you only do every once in a while. Alternatively, schedule a smaller treat as "Me Time" on a regular basis and stick to it as ongoing self-care. Choose something you wouldn't do ordinarily or that you do rarely. Or perhaps it's something you do already but you want to do it in a different way. (Even grocery shopping at a different time on your own can be seen as a treat, if doing it with children at peak hours is your usual mode of operation. Remember, it all depends on your context!)

The important thing about a treat is that it has to be experienced mindfully. What's the point of scheduling yourself a treat if you're not going to pay attention while doing it?

Mindful Treat

What to Do:

1. Before you actually begin your treat, close your eyes and take a bit of time to be in the moment. Let all the things that have been dogging you melt away; it's just you and whatever you've chosen as your treat. In your mind, say, *"This time is mine; I declare it so."*

2. Take the time to really enjoy all the dimensions of your treat. Watch people; notice the scents of the area you're in; taste things mindfully; enjoy the sensations of turning pages or discovering the story in your book or on your e-reader.

3. If you can't fully settle into your treat time, don't force it. And don't allow yourself to be irritated that it isn't as special as you want it to be. Not every moment of your self-care will be blissful. But it will be time spent doing what you have chosen to do, and that's important.

Tip:

♦ Naturally, mindfulness will be different if you're in a crowd or with a group of friends for your treat. Adjust your expectations and roll on!

Clear Your Energy

An important aspect of physical self-care is hygiene. Washing your face, showering or bathing, brushing your hair...all these serve to keep you clean and tidy. The same sort of attention should be paid to your personal energy. Your aura or personal energy field can collect all sorts of unwanted grit and murky energy. Keeping it tidy means you're tending to its well-being.

Clearing Energy Debris

It's never a bad time to shake up the negative energy that has collected around your aura. Brush off the cobwebs with this visualization!

Note: Banishing is usually associated with a counterclockwise movement. Try this visualization with the wind flowing around you counterclockwise first. If it feels odd, try it with the wind circling clockwise around you instead. Or try each and make notes on the differences, then choose a direction in the future that best suits the results you're looking for at that particular moment.

What to Do:

1. Ground and center.
2. Imagine wind, warm wind. Hear it; feel it stir your hair, your clothing. Let it increase until it plays around you in a gentle cyclonelike motion. Imagine it polishing off the dull, murky spots on your aura, flaking away any negative energy that has built up on it. Let the wind play around your aura until you feel that the energy is clean.

Be Open to Receiving Love

It sounds obvious, but a lot of the time our thought patterns or subconscious guilt or beliefs about ourselves push love away. The following spell affirms that you are open to receiving love and self-care.

Receive Love

This spell is one you may have to perform on a regular basis to remind yourself and reaffirm that you are open to receiving love, both from others and yourself.

What You Need:

- Matches or a lighter
- Rose or jasmine incense and a censer
- 6 pink candles and candleholders (tea lights or birthday candles work well)
- Rose quartz stone
- Pen or marker

What to Do:

1. Center and ground.
2. Light the incense.
3. Place one candle in the center of your work space. Place one to each side and slightly behind it. Set the next two slightly in front and to either side of the first candle (a bit closer than the previous two). Place the final candle in front of the first candle, closer to you than the previous two. The candles should be in the rough shape of a heart.
4. Hold the rose quartz between your hands, saying, *"I am receptive to love and care. I welcome love."*

5. Place the rose quartz in the center of the heart shape. Begin to light the candles, saying as you light each one, *"I welcome love. I deserve love. I am loved."*

6. Stay there for a bit, feeling love surround you and feeling love for the universe. You can allow the candles to burn out before you wrap up (easier with the birthday candles; tea lights burn for 4–6 hours), or snuff the candles and incense out and keep them for the next time you do this spell. (Once they're cool, slip them into a zip-top bag and label it.) Carry the rose quartz with you.

Create a Treasure Bag for Self-Care

Some of the spells in this book will suggest that you carry stones, small pouches, written things, and so forth with you. It might get a bit unwieldy having all those things lurking at the bottom of your briefcase or backpack. Why not make a treasure bag for them, a pouch that serves as a master container for all the magical self-care odds and ends?

Self-Care Treasure Bag

You can use any kind of fabric you like for this treasure bag, but avoid really light fabrics like chiffon or gauze. You can scale the size up or down too. This version makes a pouch roughly 7" × 4".

What You Need:

* 2 rectangles of fabric, approximately 8" × 10" each
* Sewing straight pins
* Scissors
* Sewing needle and thread (color of your choice)
* Iron and ironing board
* Strip of ribbon, about 8" long (approximately ¼" wide)

What to Do:

1. Place the two rectangles of fabric right sides together, lining up the edges. Pin the layers of fabric together along the two longer sides. Cut one of the short ends of the rectangles into a shallow point, about 1" deep; this will be the flap of the pouch. Pin the edges of this closed as well.

2. Sew the two long sides and the point closed with a running stitch, leaving about a ¼" seam allowance.

3. Turn the pouch inside out.

4. Iron the seams. Fold about ½" of the open end to the inside all around and iron that as well. Pin the opening together. Sew the open end closed with a running stitch.

5. Fold the bottom up, lining up the corners just under where the angle of the flap begins. Pin in place, and sew up the sides.

6. Cut the ribbon into two equal pieces. On the inside of the point, sew one end of a piece of ribbon. Fold the flap down and make note of where the point rests against the front of the pouch. About an inch below that, sew the end of the second piece of ribbon.

7. To use, slip your magical self-care objects inside. Tie closed with the ribbons.

Tips:

* If you have a sewing machine, you can use it instead of hand-sewing the seams.

- You can use fabric paint to decorate your pouch, or add iron-on or sew-on patches, or sew pretty buttons on it. A decorative button on the point of the flap will cover any stitches that show through from sewing on the ribbon.
- You can draw magical symbols on it, too, to reinforce health, protection, or other areas. Check out my book *Protection Spells* for ideas!

Be Willing to Accept Failure

Being willing to accept failure is incredibly difficult. It means you have to admit that success is not guaranteed and that you might fail even if you do all the right things.

But being willing to fail means that you get to take risks that could yield amazing outcomes. And one of the things you need to understand is that a mistake isn't failure. It's proof that you're trying, and every time you try, you learn a little more about whatever it is that you're hoping to accomplish. Bonus: you learn a little more about yourself as well. Everything is a learning experience. It may not necessarily be an enjoyable experience, but it's always valuable.

Spell to Be Willing to Risk Failure

The fear of failure can paralyze you. The reluctance to make decisions or take steps can often be traced back to the fear of failing in some way. To succeed, however, you have to accept the risk of failure, as well as the risk of success. Sometimes that, too, can be a scary prospect. To help yourself be more willing to risk failure, try this spell.

What You Need:

- Small bowl
- Tiger's eye stone
- Pinch crumbled or ground sage
- Pinch crumbled or ground cinnamon
- Pinch dried rose petals
- 1 drop bergamot essential oil
- 1 drop pine essential oil
- 1 drop neroli essential oil

What to Do:

1. Cleanse your supplies according to your preferred method (see Chapter 1).
2. Center and ground.
3. Set the bowl in the center of your work space.
4. Place the tiger's eye in the bowl, saying, *"Tiger's eye, bring me confidence and strength."*
5. Place the pinch of sage in the bowl, saying, *"Sage, share with me your wisdom."*
6. Place the pinch of cinnamon in the bowl, saying, *"Cinnamon, lend me spiritual growth."*
7. Place the pinch of dried rose in the bowl, saying, *"Rose, strengthen my self-acceptance."*
8. Add the drop of bergamot oil, saying, *"Bergamot, bring clarity of mind."*
9. Add the drop of pine oil, saying, *"Pine, reinforce my inner strength."*
10. Add the drop of neroli, saying, *"Neroli, deepen my inner calm."*
11. Stir the blend with a finger. Hold your hands over it, visualizing energy being drawn up from the earth, through your core, and down to your hands. Imagine the blend glowing with white light.

12. Say:

> *I am secure in myself; I have the confidence to risk failure.*
> *I am blessed with optimism and value my abilities.*
> *Failure is not a reflection of my value as a person.*
> *If this is not to be at this moment, I gain valuable insight*
> *And grow in strength and wisdom.*

13. Remove the tiger's eye and carry it with you. Sprinkle the rest of the blend outdoors.

Finding Equilibrium

If you feel buffeted by change or uncertainty, a spell to reinforce your equilibrium can help. This is good for emotional equilibrium as well as general balance in your life.

The blue lace agate in this spell carries energies associated with calm, balance, and composure, while the rhodochrosite represents comfort, balance, and stability.

Spell for Equilibrium

The quickest and easiest way to access a method of rebalancing is to center, ground, and either shunt off excess energy to the earth or draw what you need up to replace missing energy in your own system. This spell is a different approach.

What You Need:

- Pale blue or pale lavender candle and candleholder
- Matches or lighter
- Blue lace agate stone
- Rhodochrosite stone

What to Do:

1. Cleanse the stones according to your preferred method (see Chapter 1).
2. Center and ground.
3. Light the candle.
4. Hold one stone in each hand. Close your eyes and feel the weight in your palms. Slowly start to gently rock back and forth, lifting one hand while lowering the other. Keep the movement very slight at first. While you rock, say:

    Flow, ebb,
    Ebb, flow.
    Bring me balance,
    Stability show.

5. As you chant, increase your movement, bringing your body into play as well. Keep chanting until you feel your energy peak.
6. Focus on the stones again and slow your movement incrementally until you are standing still with your eyes closed, a stone in each cupped hand. Feel the sense of floating and lightness you now have. Murmur the chant one final time, then open your eyes.
7. Allow the candle to burn out. Keep the stones and reuse them whenever you need to.

Accepting Your Limits

Like it or not, you can't do everything. This spell helps you accept that you have limits, that you cannot take everything on. Boundaries exist to help keep us healthy, and establishing them— then defending them!—is a valuable part of self-care. Not only do you have to defend them from other people, sometimes you have to defend them from yourself. It's very easy to think, *Oh, I'll just do this one little thing*, and then suddenly it's been a hundred little instances of "just this" and you're wondering why you feel like you're falling apart.

> The obsidian in this spell, while excellent at repelling negativity, also helps you get in touch with your shadow side. If you are unconsciously sabotaging your own limits, using obsidian may help you recognize that.

Spell to Help Accept Limits

Sometimes you're supposed to stop; sometimes you're supposed to understand that overextending yourself is a bad plan. This spell helps you accept your limits.

What You Need:

- A photo or item representing yourself
- White candle and candleholder
- Matches or lighter
- 4 obsidian stones
- 4 hematite stones
- 1 labradorite stone
- Salt

What to Do:

1. Cleanse your supplies according to your preferred method (see Chapter 1).
2. Center and ground.
3. Set your photo in the center of your work space. Place the candle a few inches behind it.

4. Light the candle, saying, *"I illuminate my boundaries and see them clearly."*

5. Place the obsidian stones around the photo on a square, one at each corner. (The obsidians in the top corners should be between the photo and the candle.) Say, *"My limits defend me."*

6. Place the hematites around the photo as well, between each obsidian. (If your photo were a clock face, the hematites would be at 12:00, 3:00, 6:00, and 9:00.) Say, *"My limits protect me."*

7. Place the labradorite on or next to your photo or item, saying, *"My limits are strong."*

8. Sprinkle the salt in a circle around the candle, photo, and stones. Sit before the circle, repeating, *"My limits defend me; my limits protect me; my limits are strong."*

9. When you feel you are done, extinguish the candle. You may choose to cleanse the stones and return them to your supplies, or keep them with your photo somewhere safe. (Do the latter if you feel that repeating the spell regularly would benefit you.)

The Struggle of Depression

When you're depressed, pushing yourself to do things can actually be detrimental. If you'd sprained an ankle running, you wouldn't keep running on it, right? You'd take time to heal first, then start doing physical therapy to strengthen it again, and reintroduce activity little by little. A sprained ankle isn't a failure; it's a temporary setback.

Think the same way for depression. A depressive episode (or non-chronic depression, associated with stress) is a sign that you need to rest and heal. Depression is not a sign of failure in any sense of the word. It affects how your life goes, and you need to roll with that idea until you've healed.

It's also important to remember that progress in any part of your life isn't always measured by moving visibly closer to a goal. Sometimes it's defined as pausing so that you can care for yourself, or pausing to take a side quest to prepare for better success on the main path further along. Accepting that a pause may be necessary to take care of yourself as an investment in later success is an important aspect of self-care, magical and otherwise. It's especially important if you're struggling with depression.

> If you suspect that you are suffering from clinical depression, don't minimize it; please go speak to a health-care professional. Depression is a sign from your body and spirit that they need help.

Spell to Embrace Depression

Embracing doesn't mean permanent acceptance. It means under-standing that depression is a sign that you need to attend to your-self, to be extra gentle, to care for yourself. It is an essential step on the way to dealing with it and hopefully moving past it. If you know you are depressed or have been diagnosed with depression, use this spell to accept the diagnosis and remind yourself that you are worthy of love.

What You Need:

- White or gold candle in candleholder
- Matches or lighter
- White rose
- Vase with water
- Rose quartz stone

What to Do:

1. Cleanse your supplies according to your preferred method (see Chapter 1).
2. Center and ground.
3. Light the candle, saying, *"The light of my light shines in the darkness, always."*
4. Pick up the rose and hold the flower to your cheek. Close your eyes and breathe in the scent. Feel the delicacy of the petals.
5. Say:

     Delicate does not mean weak. I am worthy of love and care,
     Both from myself and others.
     I am fragile but not broken.
     I recognize that my limits have been redrawn, and accept that
     I must heal.

6. Place the rose in the vase and place the vase next to the candle.
7. Pick up the rose quartz and brush it gently against the petals of the white rose. Then bring it to your forehead and gently brush

it against your skin. Lower it to your chest and hold it against your heart.

8. Say:

> *Wounded, not dead; weak, not broken.*
> *With love and care I will heal and be stronger than before.*
> *My future is full of love and light.*

9. Place the rose quartz at the base of the candle next to the vase with the rose. Allow the candle to burn out. Carry the rose quartz with you.

Tip:

◆ When the rose begins to wilt, pull the petals off gently and use them in Making Magical Rose Beads (see Chapter 4).

The Benefits of Unplugging

While reaching out to friends can be a welcome form of support, there are times when the flurry of information and keeping up with everyone and their news and postings can make you tired. Sometimes the easiest and smartest thing to do if you're feeling overwhelmed is to unplug. Take a break from the phone, the news, social media, and electronic forms of entertainment. Explore a slower kind of relaxation.

> If you plan on taking a break from phone calls, texts, or social media, be kind and let friends know so they don't worry about you.

Unplugging helps you refocus on yourself instead of being pulled in a zillion different directions. Those directions may all be important, but you are just as important. Unplugging allows you to focus on being in the moment, here and now. It helps you step away from the emotional roller coaster that you ride reacting to a friend's story, a news article, or outrage over worldwide events. Unplugging gives you the chance to remember who you are at your core. Here are some things you can try once you shut off the noise of the news cycle and social media:

- Listen to music. This is something that is often done as an accompaniment or background to other activities. Take time to actually listen to the depth and richness of your preferred music. You may notice things you've never noticed before.

- Read something for pleasure. A physical book or magazine is ideal, but you can use an e-reader or a reading app on your smartphone or tablet as long as you disconnect from the Internet while doing it. Don't let notifications distract you, and don't let an idle *I'll just look this one thing up* derail your mindful activity time.

- Work with your hands for a bit. Draw, paint, garden, cook, bake, craft. Why not check out some of the magical and spiritual self-care activities in Chapter 4 to explore creativity, or some of the recipes in Chapter 3?

As passionate as you are about the causes you support and the freedoms you defend, sometimes trying to stay on top of the news and outreach can exhaust you. Sometimes it's best for you to step back from it all and heal your stress in order to be in tip-top shape to get back into the fight.

But not everyone has the privilege of stepping away, you might say. "How can I take the option to step out of the ring when there are people dying, starving, being oppressed?" you ask. Comparing your personal state to someone else's is a recipe for ducking out of self-care. Someone will always be worse off. That doesn't mean you should avoid taking care of yourself right now. Live to fight another day. Take time off to recharge and regroup, and bring your best self back to support your cause.

Setting Boundaries

Boundaries are an important part of self-care, helping to keep you balanced and whole. They protect you from an onslaught of energy and people claiming your time. If you have a problem saying no to people, perhaps your boundaries need to be strengthened.

In magic, we think of a personal shield as a form of energy boundary. There are other kinds of boundaries, however, that are important in self-care. We all have limits, and innate limits are there to help us defend our physical, mental, and emotional health.

Many people who practice magic, who self-identify as a witch or pagan, or who otherwise work with natural energies, also self-identify as healers in some way. When you work as a healer, you have to be very careful to set firm boundaries, otherwise you can end up lost in someone else's pain. Being there for someone and supporting them can wear you down to a point where you can't focus properly on your own affairs. You can feel tethered to your phone, reluctant to go to sleep in case someone needs you, feel guilty for forgetting about them by having a good time somewhere.

Helping friends through tough times is a wonderful, loving thing to do, but you can only do it successfully if you are in the right place to do so mentally and otherwise. Sometimes you reach a point in supporting other people where it becomes detrimental to your own health, be it emotional, spiritual, or physical. When you exhaust yourself, you need help too.

Telling someone that you need a break and drawing boundaries is incredibly difficult. Be honest and communicate clearly; explain your own situation, your own feelings. Don't feel guilty for needing space. Try using these statements to communicate your need for setting boundaries for your time and energy:

- I love you. I care for you. In order to keep helping you, I need some space to heal myself.
- I am worried that in my current state, I can't support you the way I want to. I'm concerned that I will say the wrong thing, that I will misguide you or cause more harm than good.
- There is a lot going on in my life and I can't stay on top of it.

What should you offer your friend instead of an all-access pass to your time and energy?

- Suggest time windows. Remind them that you care and that is why you are making sure that you are accessible at specific times to them.
- Suggest talking about other interests with them, not just the hard stuff.

Treating Your Inner Child

A term you may know is *inner child*, which describes the childlike aspect of an individual's identity, a semiautonomous part of your character subordinate to the waking conscious mind. Carl Jung perceived it as the child archetype, a link to a person's past self, childhood experiences, and emotion, part of the foundation of an individual's adult developed self. Popular psychology associates potential, creativity, and expression with the inner child.

As adults, sometimes we're drawn to toys or fun stuff that we certainly don't need on a practical level but that we want anyhow. We often deny ourselves indulging in this sort of fun because money has more important places to go, or because we're grown up and we don't need stupid stuff like that. And yet…we still wish.

The inner-child concept can help you explore the idea of self-care. For example, we are often very hard on ourselves, using negative self-talk or setting ridiculously high standards that we wouldn't apply to friends or children. If you catch yourself engaging in negative self-talk (*This is ridiculous; I'm so stupid; I'll never get this right*), pause and ask yourself if you would say that to a child or allow a child to say it without offering him or her emotional support. Self-care is nurturing yourself on a daily basis. If you think of the simple wants and needs of a child, perhaps doing so can give you a different perception of the kind of self-care you need.

Many sorts of little things can delight a child: a surprise ice-cream outing for no specific reason; a new pack of markers; putting shiny stickers on calendar squares when counting down to an event; going for a walk in the rain and dropping leaves into storm runoff. They may not be what your particular inner child wants or needs, but allow yourself the opportunity to think about what your inner child might enjoy. And remember to always parent your inner child with love and respect.

Comfort Objects

Did you have a beloved stuffed animal or blanket as a child, one that got battered and worn but you still carried it everywhere you could? Comfort objects like this help you transition from known situations to unknown ones by giving you a sense of continuity and of being cared for.

As adults we sometimes intentionally deprive ourselves of comfort in an odd attempt to prove that we don't need it. Using childhood comfort objects can signal nurturing to your inner child.

As an adult, there's nothing wrong with having a special object like a doll or stuffed animal that makes you feel happy or comforted when you see it. Don't go overboard—Do you really have room for an entire set of collectibles or a line of action figures?—but if there's something you want that would bring you comfort, this is the opportunity to indulge. Bonus points if you can snuggle it during self-care breaks or place it where you can see it often so it will make you smile.

Self-Care at Work

Work is a challenging place. You have to deal with the energy of many different people and work to a schedule that may not be ideal for your personal rhythms. Your workplace culture may also place unnecessary emphasis on overtime, skipping lunch, and next-to-impossible deadlines, thanks to poor scheduling or overambitious projects and not enough team members to support the work required. But there are ways to cope!

> Review the Casting a Circle exercise in Chapter 1. Use this exercise as a personal shield to help keep negative energy at arm's length. (For more techniques to defend your personal energy in the workplace, see my book *Protection Spells*.)

Positive visualization and affirmations are easy and effective techniques to help you incorporate self-care into your workday. Try incorporating timed work sessions and breaks into your day. Set alarms on your phone or activity tracker to take regular breaks to stretch and rest your eyes.

Try building a vision board specifically for work, focusing on your self-care goals in terms of the workplace. If you're shy about displaying it, make it small (around 5" × 7") and put it in a photo frame, then tell anyone who gives it an odd look that it's inspirational art.

Make a collection of items that are important to you, that inspire calm and focus when you look at them. Pick a pretty bowl or a jar, and place stones in it, small figures, and trinkets. Stones that are ideal to include are jasper for strength, clear quartz for energy, rose quartz for self-love and positive energy, amethyst for protection, and sodalite for wisdom.

Stay in the Moment

Self-care has a lot to do with being in the moment and keeping yourself from worrying about the past, the future, or things over which you have no control, such as the opinions of others. Here's a list of reminders to read now and then to keep yourself on the right track at work.

• Break larger tasks down and delegate what you can.
• Set priorities and drop the other stuff if you need to, without guilt.

- Communicate as often and as clearly as you can when you see problems looming. It's better to alert people that you'll be a day late delivering something than to overwork yourself hitting the initial deadline and render yourself useless for the next few days.

- Set boundaries and stick to them. Say no when someone asks you to help with something if you don't have the time.

- Be organized. Disorder not only creates chaotic energy, it makes it harder to keep track of what your priorities are and the material you need to meet your goals.

- Outline short-term goals, or break larger goals down into a series of short-term goals. The pleasure you obtain from making smaller goals will carry you forward to the next task. Celebrate hitting goals too.

- Remember that things don't need to be perfect. They just need to be good enough.

- Remember to breathe deeply now and then to replenish your oxygen levels and help release tension in your body.

Mini Self-Care Disconnection to Re-Center at Work

Being at work can make being mindful and taking time for yourself a challenge. Here's a quick 5-minute activity to help you disconnect and re-center yourself. You can even do it on the way to the restroom; pick one on another floor to change up the things you see.

What to Do:

1. Either at lunchtime or on a break, go for a short walk. If you work in a high-rise, go down to the lobby; bonus points if you take the stairs there or back for all or part of the way.
2. As you walk, notice your breathing; observe your inhalation and exhalation without judgment.
3. Look at the things around you; notice the colors, the textures, the quality of light.
4. Return to your work space. Sit down and close your eyes. Take three deep, slow breaths. As you exhale each time, allow yourself to release any tension your body is carrying.
5. Return to work. You've just changed your mental and physical space for 5 minutes. Even that brief mental break, paired with physical movement and being mindful, can help you reset your mind.

Tip:

• Are you in the habit of working through lunch and/or eating at your desk? You may think you get more work done that way, but it might actually not be true. Not allowing your brain and body a chance to be somewhere different can actually slow you down later in the day. Sometimes the adage "A change is as good as a rest" has meaning! Stepping away from your desk allows you to get out of your regular environment, which can help reset your mind. Eating in a different place allows you to appreciate your food more. It's hard to be mindful when your focus is on work. You deserve time away from your desk.

Chapter 3

Physical Self-Care

Physical health is an important element of self-care. Respect your body by nourishing it, caring for it, and celebrating it. Your body is the vehicle that houses your spirit, and deserves honor for that. A healthy relationship with your body strengthens and supports the self-care work you do to keep your mind and spirit healthy. Self-esteem, self-love, and well-being are all intertwined, and the physical body often is shunted lower on the list of priorities when it comes to self-care. Topics like food, aging, clothing choice, rest, and exercise can carry uncomfortable associations rooted in past expectations or experiences, and make it hard for you to accept and love your physical body. You are worth it. The physical body is an important part of you and your self-care regime. This chapter explores ways to approach caring for the physical body.

Stress and the Physical Body

High levels of stress can lead to an overtaxed immune system and is said to reduce the efficiency at which you digest food and extract nutrients from it. Stress interrupts sleep or lowers the quality of it. Stress leads to taking poor self-care, and that's something that needs to change in order to keep yourself in optimal shape physically and otherwise.

If you have access to medical professionals and decent medical insurance, don't ignore the opportunity for annual medical and dental checkups. Catching potential problems before they become major issues can save you a lot of grief. If you are struggling with depression, anxiety, or an inordinate amount of stress, take those issues to your medical professional as well. Remember, these things are not weaknesses or failures; they're symptoms of your body's systems not working to optimal efficiency.

Remember to Hydrate

How can you forget something so simple as drinking water? Easily. You reach for caffeine to help you perk up and stay awake; you reach for soda for sweetness; you drink smoothies to maximize your protein or fruit-and-vegetable intake. (Okay, that last one isn't so bad.) But most people do need a lot more plain water than they actually drink.

How do you remind yourself to drink water? Try this spell for making and programming a reusable cup to help you hydrate more and bring good health toward you.

Making a Magical Water Bottle

Even better than just purchasing and using a pretty cup is programming a container to draw health and happiness toward you, providing positive energy to draw into your body with every sip!

What You Need:

- Reusable bottle or cup with lid and straw
- Blank sheet of paper (8" × 10")
- Clear quartz crystal stone
- Rose quartz stone
- Sharpie marker (permanent ink)

What to Do:

1. Before you start, wash and dry the bottle or cup.
2. Center and ground.
3. Lay the blank piece of paper in the center of your work space. Place the bottle in the center of the paper. Place the clear quartz crystal a couple of inches behind the cup, and the rose quartz a couple of inches in front of it. With the Sharpie, draw an arrow leading from the clear quartz to the bottle, then from the bottle to the rose quartz. Draw a final arrow from the rose quartz pointing to you.
4. Say:

   Bottle, be for me an element in caring for my optimal health.
   Deliver hydration so that my body's thirst is quenched,
   So that my skin glows,
   So that my body is washed clean of toxins.
   Each sip draws happiness to me. I drink in joy and positive energy.
   It is so!

5. Pick up the bottle, turn it over, and write your name on the bottom of it. Say, "*With this I seal the spell.*"
6. Bring it to work, and hydrate, hydrate, hydrate!

Rest Your Eyes

This is one of those things that we forget to do a lot. Use this exercise as the perfect way to take a couple of minutes out and reconnect with your inner self as well as rest your eyes.

Exercise: Rest Your Eyes

What to Do:

1. Center and ground. Close your eyes.
2. Breathe slowly and deeply five times, then begin repeating this affirmation (either aloud or in your head): *"I am relaxed and focused. I see clearly."*
3. Continue breathing and repeating the affirmation for 2–3 minutes.
4. Open your eyes. Flex your hands and feet, then stretch your arms and legs. Roll your neck gently. Return to work.

Nutrition As Self-Care

Proper eating habits are often the first things to go out the window when we are stressed. Perhaps you drop eating almost entirely because of time constraints or lack of appetite (guilty as charged). Or maybe your food intake gets shunted lower on your list of priorities, shoehorned in between other things on your to-do list, and you eat what is easy instead of what is optimal for your best care, or you eat quickly because there's no more time.

But eating is one of the most basic forms of self-care there is. Without adequate nutrition, you become incapable of handling your other daily tasks. Fatigue and low energy levels are all too common results. Your memory and mental clarity can also suffer. Essentially, you undermine your basic functioning. This isn't even about eating the right kinds of food; this is about covering your body's basic needs to function.

Food also impacts mood. Mood is regulated by hormone production, which takes a hit when you short yourself on food that has adequate nutritional value. Listen to your body's needs in regard to food. Ever been hungry because you didn't provide your body with enough fuel? Or been lethargic and unable to focus because you've eaten a meal that was too big?

> Food can be tricky. Sometimes we get caught up in using food to reward ourselves or as self-care in a less-than-constructive way, trying to cheer ourselves up with treats that may make us feel good emotionally but that don't pack as great a reward for our nutritional levels. And sometimes, when you feel like most of your life is out of control, eating food becomes something that you can control. Remember, an extravagant food-based treat once in a while can be indulgent, but indulge too often, and it's no longer a treat.

Energy is required to invest in food planning and preparation, which can be daunting if you are already struggling with anxiety, depression, a crazy schedule, or low energy levels. Your living conditions and income may not allow for proper food storage or preparation, which can also impact your ability to manage nutritional self-care.

There's no magic bullet to fix problems with food. But you should do what you can whenever you can. To make planning easier, take half an hour a week to plan out meals so you're not caught half an hour before dinner wondering what to make. Order groceries online if you can; if not, make sure you have a master list of everything you'll need to make that week's meals. To make prepping easier, make extra and freeze some for days when you come home late and need to eat but have zero energy.

Recipes

Fair warning: this section of the self-care book isn't overly concerned with calorie counting. The recipes are not extravagant, but they don't cut corners either. They are about comfort, about feeling good.

Soups

Soups are a wonderful self-care food. They're thick and filling and warm and soft. And they're also easy to make and easy to freeze. If they're too thick when you defrost them, add more broth.

Roasted-Vegetable Soup

This is my favorite kind of fall soup! It's a great way to celebrate the harvest. Carrots are associated with success (especially physical success); squash, with blessing and awareness of other realms; peppers carry protective energy; tomatoes are associated with health, love, and protection; sweet potatoes are associated with love; and onions and garlic, with protection.

This recipe serves 6.

What You Need:

- 1 large onion, peeled
- 8 medium carrots, peeled
- 1 small butternut squash, peeled and seeded
- 4 medium red bell peppers, stemmed and seeded
- 3 large tomatoes, seeded
- 4 medium sweet potatoes, peeled
- 4 large parsnips, peeled

- 2 tablespoons olive oil
- 1 tablespoon chopped fresh rosemary
- 1 teaspoon salt
- ½ teaspoon freshly ground black pepper
- ½ head garlic, cloves peeled
- 5 cups stock (chicken or vegetable)

1. Preheat the oven to 425°F.
2. Chop the vegetables into 2" chunks.
3. In a large bowl, toss the vegetables with the olive oil and then spread on a large baking dish. Sprinkle with the rosemary and add salt and pepper.
4. Place in the oven and roast for 1 hour. Then add the garlic cloves, stir, and return to the oven for another 45 minutes.
5. Remove from the oven and transfer vegetables to a large bowl. Pour stock into the roasting pan and deglaze it, scraping up any gooey or browned bits. Pour the stock into the bowl with the roasted vegetables.
6. If you have a blender, liquidize the soup in small batches and pour the purée into a large saucepan. Otherwise, put the vegetables and stock directly into the pan and use an immersion blender to purée the soup. Thin the consistency out with more stock, if desired. If it's too thin, let it simmer longer to evaporate some of the extra liquid. Taste and adjust seasoning to your preference.
7. Serve hot with fresh bread. You can add a dollop of sour cream or Greek yogurt to your bowl of soup, if you like.

Leek and Potato Soup

Leeks are underrated. Potatoes carry protective energy, while leeks are part of the onion family, associated with health and clearing negativity. For a dairy-free, vegan version, replace the butter with olive oil, and use coconut milk instead of the whole milk.

This recipe serves 4.

What You Need:

- 2 medium leeks, sliced lengthwise and soaked
- 2 tablespoons butter
- 1 small onion, peeled and chopped
- 4 cups stock (chicken or vegetable)
- 8 medium potatoes, peeled and cubed
- 1 bay leaf
- 1 sprig fresh thyme
- ½ teaspoon salt
- ½ teaspoon freshly ground black pepper
- 1 cup whole milk
- Heavy cream (optional)
- 2 tablespoons minced chives or green onions
- Grated Cheddar cheese (optional)

1. Remove the root end of the leek and chop the light green and white parts only, discarding the dark-green tops.
2. Melt the butter in a large, heavy saucepan over medium heat. Cook the leeks and onion till soft, stirring regularly (about 10 minutes).
3. Pour stock into the pan, stirring up any browning from the bottom. Add potatoes, bay leaf, thyme, salt, and pepper, and stir again. Reduce heat to medium-low and simmer about 25 minutes.
4. Stir in milk and simmer another 15 minutes. Remove the bay leaf and the sprig of thyme. Use an immersion blender to purée the soup in the pan, or purée it in batches in a standard blender. If the soup is too thin, simmer till thicker; if too thick, add a bit of stock. Stir in a bit of heavy cream for a more luxurious soup, if you like.

5. Top with minced chives and serve with fresh bread.

6. If you like cheese with your potatoes, stir in a cup of shredded Cheddar cheese until it's melted for an extra treat.

Gazpacho

A delicious, cool, smooth summery treat! Float homemade Parmesan croutons on top for an extra treat (see following recipe). If your tomatoes aren't very juicy, you can add a bit of tomato or vegetable juice to the bread and vegetable mixture to help moisten them.

This recipe serves 4.

What You Need:

- 1 medium cucumber, peeled and chopped
- 1 medium red bell pepper, stemmed, seeded, and chopped
- 1 medium green bell pepper, stemmed, seeded, and chopped
- 2 pounds plum or Roma tomatoes, chopped
- 2 cloves garlic, peeled and minced
- ¼ cup peeled, chopped red onion
- 4 slices stale white bread (preferably country-loaf style), torn into cubes
- 2 tablespoons olive oil
- 2 tablespoons rice-wine vinegar
- 1 tablespoon fresh lemon juice
- ½ teaspoon salt
- ½ teaspoon freshly ground black pepper
- 2 tablespoons fresh basil, chopped (for garnish)

1. Toss the chopped vegetables and the bread together in a large bowl. Sprinkle the olive oil, vinegar, lemon juice, salt, and pepper over it all, then toss again. Press down to release the juices of the vegetables, then cover with plastic wrap and place in the refrigerator at least 1 hour (overnight is ideal).
2. Transfer the chilled ingredients to a food processor or blender and purée. If you want it to be smoother and less chunky, add up to 2 more tablespoons olive oil, a little at a time, blending well between each addition.
3. Taste and add a splash more vinegar, salt, and pepper, if desired. Cover and refrigerate again until well chilled.
4. Serve sprinkled with chopped fresh basil.

Parmesan Croutons

These are lovely in gazpacho or in a salad—or eaten by themselves, honestly. If your bread is fresh and not slightly stale, place the slices of bread in a 300°F oven for 1–2 minutes to dry them out slightly before cutting them into cubes. You can use any kind of bread for these. It's a great way to use up stale bread. You can also substitute melted butter for the olive oil.

What You Need:

- 4 thick slices country bread, slightly stale
- 4 tablespoons olive oil
- 2 teaspoons grated Parmesan cheese
- Pinch dried oregano
- Pinch dried basil
- Pinch dried thyme
- Pinch garlic powder
- Sprinkle of salt

1. Preheat the oven to 300°F. Line a baking sheet with aluminum foil or baking parchment.
2. Cut the crusts off the slices of bread, if desired. Cut the bread into small cubes.
3. In a medium bowl, mix the olive oil, Parmesan cheese, oregano, basil, thyme, garlic powder, and salt. Add the bread cubes and toss to coat.
4. Transfer cubes to the lined baking sheet and bake about 20 minutes until golden brown. Cool completely before serving or transferring to storage container of your choice.

Breads

The thing I love to bake most of all is bread. I apologize for the delicious smells that emanate from my house on a regular basis to all of you nearby who function best on high-protein, low-carb diets.

Grains are magically associated with abundance and prosperity.

Basic White Bread

This is the current version of my go-to basic bread. It slices well for sandwiches. I use a stand mixer to knead my regular weekly bread, although I will make magical breads by hand to infuse them with specific energy. This is a wet dough that works well in a stand mixer.

This recipe yields 2 loaves.

What You Need:

+ 2 teaspoons active dry yeast
+ Pinch sugar
+ 1 teaspoon salt

+ 1 tablespoon plus 2 teaspoons vegetable oil, divided
+ 2 cups warm water
+ 5 cups bread flour

Flour Substitutions

You can substitute up to half whole-wheat flour for the bread flour. You may need a bit of extra liquid to account for it. Add the whole-wheat flour first, and let it sit for a bit to absorb some liquid before adding the rest of the bread flour and mixing. You may want to let it rise a bit longer too.

1. Combine yeast, sugar, salt, 1 tablespoon oil, and water in a medium bowl. Allow the yeast to activate and become foamy, which can take 5–10 minutes.

2. Stir in 2 cups flour, then add the remaining flour cup by cup. If the dough is still very sticky and you are unable to handle it, add extra flour a little bit at a time. The dough shouldn't be dry, however.

3. Turn dough out onto a lightly floured surface and knead for 5–8 minutes. The dough is damp; the extra water means you don't have to knead it as much. Use just enough flour to keep it from being a mess.

4. Oil the inside of the bowl with 1 teaspoon oil and return the dough to the bowl, turning to coat the entire surface with oil. Cover the bowl with a damp cloth and put it inside an unheated oven to rise about 1 hour.

5. Remove the dough from the oven and punch it down, folding a couple of times.

6. Lightly oil the inside of two loaf pans with the remaining 1 teaspoon oil. Cut the dough in half and shape each half into a loaf. Lay them in the pans, turning to coat with oil again. Put the loaves in the unheated oven and allow them to rise 30 minutes more.

7. Remove the pans from the oven. Preheat the oven to 350°F.

8. Place loaves in heated oven and bake 30 minutes until golden brown on top. Remove from pans; the bottoms should sound hollow when knocked after being tipped out of the pans. If the bottoms are soft or the knock is heavy instead of hollow, return them to the oven for a few minutes then check again. Allow to cool on a rack.

Herb Rolls

When I've made these, my kids will ignore the sandwich bread and use these for sandwiches and snacks instead. And I can't blame them. They're lovely with a wedge of cheese.

This recipe yields approximately 16 rolls.

What You Need:

- 1 teaspoon active dry yeast
- Pinch sugar
- 1/2 teaspoon salt
- 4 teaspoons melted butter, divided
- 1 cup warm water
- 2 1/2 cups all-purpose flour
- 1/2 teaspoon garlic powder
- 1/2 teaspoon onion powder
- 1 teaspoon minced fresh chives
- 1 teaspoon Italian seasoning (basil, rosemary, thyme, marjoram, oregano)
- 2 teaspoons vegetable oil, to coat bowl and pan

1. Combine yeast, sugar, salt, 2 teaspoons melted butter, and water in a medium bowl. Allow the yeast to activate and become foamy, which can take 5–10 minutes.
2. Stir in 1 cup flour, stir in the seasonings, then add the remaining flour in two parts. If the dough is still very sticky, add extra flour a little bit at a time to allow it to be handled. The dough shouldn't be dry, however.
3. Turn out onto a lightly floured surface and knead 5–8 minutes. The dough is damp; use just enough flour to keep it from being a mess.

4. Oil the inside of the bowl with 1 teaspoon of oil and return the dough to it, turning to coat the entire surface with oil. Cover the bowl with a damp cloth and put it inside an unheated oven to rise, about 1 hour.

5. Remove dough from the oven and punch it down, folding a couple of times.

6. Lightly oil a baking sheet or flat pan with the remaining oil. Twist off knobs of dough and shape them into your preferred size (I like about 1½" diameter balls). Lay them on the pan, barely touching one another, in neat rows. Brush the tops with remaining melted butter. Put the pan in the unheated oven and allow the rolls to rise 45 minutes more.

7. Remove the pan from the oven. Preheat the oven to 350°F.

8. Place the rolls in heated oven and bake 30 minutes, until golden brown on top. Allow the rolls to cool on a rack.

Main Dishes and Sides

The core of your meal! The first two recipes are classic comfort foods, and the potato recipe pairs with just about everything.

Pot Roast

Meat carries life energy, as does red wine (which you might choose to use in this recipe). Garlic and onions are associated with good health. The protein in meat also serves to ground you. If you can, experiment with using grass-fed or free-pastured beef. The flavor is truly a revelation. Serve this over mashed potatoes with carrot coins sautéed quickly in butter.

This recipe serves 4.

What You Need:

- 3 pounds boneless blade roast
- 1 teaspoon salt
- 1 teaspoon freshly ground pepper
- 3 large cloves garlic, peeled and finely minced
- 2 tablespoons Montreal steak seasoning
- 2 tablespoons olive oil, divided
- 2 small yellow or red onions, peeled and diced
- 1 cup sliced white button mushrooms
- 1 cup beef broth
- 1 cup red or white wine
- 2 teaspoons cornstarch

1. Rub the roast with the salt and pepper, garlic, and Montreal steak seasoning. Allow it to sit about 1 hour at room temperature.

2. Pour 1 tablespoon olive oil into a deep, wide saucepot or a Dutch oven and heat it on the stovetop over medium-high heat. Add the roast and sear it on all sides. Remove roast and allow it to stand on a plate while you do the next step.

3. Reduce the heat to medium-low. Add the remaining tablespoon olive oil and sauté the onions till soft. (If the residue on the bottom of the pan gets too brown, reduce the heat further, add a bit of water, and scrape it up into the onions.) Add the mushrooms and stir, sautéing a bit longer. Pour in the beef broth and wine and stir, scraping up the crunchy bits from the bottom.

4. Place the roast back into the pot and pour in any juices that have accumulated while it rested.

5. Cover the pot and reduce heat to just above minimum. Allow roast to cook about 2 hours, then carefully flip it. Cover the pot again and allow roast to cook another 2 hours.

6. Test the roast by pulling some apart with two forks; if it shreds easily and is moist inside, it's done. If it's hard to pull apart, cover it again and let it cook longer. Check every 10 minutes, adding a bit more wine or broth if necessary. When the meat is easily shredded, remove about ¼ cup of the cooking liquid to a small bowl and whisk in the cornstarch.

7. Push the meat to one side of the pot. Raise the heat to medium-high and stir in the cornstarch mixture; allow it to come to a boil to thicken the gravy. Taste the gravy and adjust seasoning if necessary. Turn off the heat and shred the rest of the pot roast with forks in the pot. Serve hot.

Baked Macaroni and Cheese

This is nice when made with whole-wheat pasta; the nuttiness of the pasta complements the cheese sauce nicely. Undercooking the pasta just a tad allows it to remain firmer and hold its own against the cheese sauce. Dairy products are associated with nourishment and health, and grain products are associated with prosperity and abundance.

This recipe serves 5.

What You Need:

* 8 ounces regular or whole-wheat pasta (rotini, fusilli, or shape of your choice)
* 1 teaspoon plus 3 tablespoons plus 1½ tablespoons butter, divided
* ¼ cup flour
* 2½ cups milk
* ½ teaspoon salt
* ¼ teaspoon freshly ground black pepper
* Pinch onion powder
* Pinch garlic powder
* 1 cup shredded Gruyère cheese
* 1 cup shredded Gouda cheese (preferably smoked)
* 1 cup shredded Oka or Port Salut cheese (or other semisoft smooth and creamy cheese)
* 1 cup shredded sharp Cheddar
* ½ cup bread crumbs (panko is ideal)

Experiment with Flavors
In addition to the spices called for in this recipe, you could also add a pinch or two of herbes de Provence and a dab of Dijon mustard, or a pinch of nutmeg. Enjoy experimenting!

1. Preheat oven to 350°F.

2. Cook the pasta according to the package directions but for 1 minute less than indicated. Drain, return to the pan, and stir in 1 teaspoon butter.

3. In another large saucepan, melt the 3 tablespoons butter over medium heat. Stir in the flour and cook 1 minute, stirring constantly.

4. Pour in 1 cup milk and whisk to combine the paste with the liquid. Add the remaining milk and keep whisking. Add the salt and pepper, onion powder, and garlic powder and cook approximately 5 minutes, stirring constantly, until the sauce has thickened to a creamy consistency. Remove from the heat and stir in the grated cheeses. Check seasoning and adjust if necessary.

5. Pour sauce over pasta and stir together gently. Pour into a baking dish.

6. In a small bowl, use a fork to blend together the bread crumbs and 1½ tablespoons butter. Sprinkle over top of the macaroni.

7. Bake about 30 minutes. Don't overbake; this is supposed to be creamy!

Rosemary Potatoes

I love how potatoes get sweet when you roast them. I use Russets when I can, but Yukon Gold or other yellow-fleshed potatoes also work in this recipe. Rosemary and lemon brighten them nicely.

This recipe serves 4.

What You Need:

- 1 pound mini potatoes
- 1 tablespoon olive oil plus 1 teaspoon
- 1 tablespoon Dijon mustard
- 2 teaspoons chopped fresh rosemary
- 2 teaspoons lemon juice
- 1 clove garlic, peeled and minced
- 1 teaspoon salt
- ½ teaspoon freshly ground black pepper
- Pinch cayenne pepper

1. Preheat oven to 425°F. Line a baking sheet with aluminum foil and brush with a teaspoon of olive oil.
2. Cut potatoes in half; larger ones can be quartered. Place in a large bowl and add the rest of the ingredients. Stir well to coat.
3. Spread the potatoes on the baking sheet and place in the oven. Roast 15 minutes, stir, turning the potatoes over, and roast another 15 minutes or until a knife inserted slips in easily and the insides are tender. Serve.

The Benefits of Teas

Tea offers physical benefits beyond the comforting feel of a warm cup in your hand or a shot of caffeine. L-theanine is a nondietary amino acid found in tea leaves. L-theanine encourages relaxation and promotes dopamine levels. It's a compound that relieves stress and affects brain-wave patterns to behave as they do when the body is relaxed, raising alpha-frequency waves to foster an alert, calm state. It's found in both green and black teas, with levels highest in green tea like matcha.

Note that you should research any herb before using it in a tea. Check interactions with any medications that you already use and any possible contraindications for your existing allergies.

Here are some common components of herbal teas and information about them.

Chamomile

Daisylike plants from the Asteraceae family, the chamomile used in medicinal and herbal applications is most commonly Roman chamomile (*Chamaemelum nobile*) and German chamomile (*Matricaria chamomilla*). Chamomile tea is often used for antianxiety, its sedative effect, and the promotion of relaxation in general. (It should not be used by pregnant women, as it can trigger uterine contractions.)

Lavender

If there is a classic herb associated with serenity, relaxation, and calm, it's lavender (*Lavandula angustifolia*). It's particularly good for addressing emotional stress, although it functions for physical and mental stress as well. Try adding a pinch of lavender flowers to any black tea, or blend it with chamomile, verbena, and a bit of mint for a pleasant, destressing herbal tea.

Lemon Balm

Lemon balm (*Melissa officinalis*) has relaxing properties that help soothe headaches, calm anxiety, and treat insomnia. It's good to take when you're coming down with a cold, too, as it has antiviral properties. The flavor is delicate and lemony.

Lemon Verbena

Lemon verbena (*Aloysia citriodora*, also called *Lippia citriodora*) promotes restful sleep, works as an anti-inflammatory, improves digestion, calms nerves, eases stress, and functions as an antioxidant. The flavor is fresh and lemony.

Passion Flower

Passion flower (*Passiflora* spp.) combats anxiety, panic, insomnia, and depression. It also has analgesic properties, which means it calms nerve pain. It can help balance mood as well. The taste is mild and fresh. Pregnant women should avoid passion flower, as it can stimulate uterine contractions.

Skullcap

American skullcap (*Scutellaria lateriflora*) is used to treat anxiety, headaches, and insomnia. It's a nervine that promotes relaxation and a sense of well-being in the face of stress. (Make sure the skullcap you use is American skullcap; Chinese skullcap (*Scutellaria baicalensis*) is an entirely different plant with different applications.)

Vervain

Vervain (*Verbena officinalis*) possesses an antianxiety, relaxant, sedative effect, as well as functioning as a strong antioxidant; it packs a lot of vitamin C. The taste can be bitter, so it's good to mix it with other herbs or add some lemon and honey. Note: Thanks to its botanical name, vervain is sometimes confused with verbena (see earlier entry).

Bath and Shower Care

Hygiene is a necessity, but there's no reason why you can't max out the enjoyment at the same time! Self-care can include the basic level of hygiene, just as it can include the basics of eating food to survive. But turning it into an enjoyable experience and a special moment…that's magical, and it really nourishes the soul beyond simply the body.

Add special energy to your baths and showers by making and using magical mixtures like these scrub bars, bath bombs, bath oils, and bath salts.

Shower Scrub Bars

Sugar scrubs are decadent but can get a bit goopy sitting in a jar. Why not try a sugar-scrub cube or bar instead? This blend has oils and beeswax to nourish the skin, and superfine or castor sugar to help gently slough off dead skin cells. If you don't have superfine sugar, run regular granulated sugar through your blender or food processor to reduce the size of the granules. You can add grated lemon zest to the mixture before you add the sugar as well. Start with a teaspoon of zest; if you decide you want a stronger lemon smell, add more. Shea butter and beeswax may be found at health food stores, or ordered online.

What You Need:

- 2½ tablespoons coconut oil
- 2 teaspoons shea butter
- 2 tablespoons beeswax granules
- Chopstick or craft stick
- 10 drops rose essential-oil blend (see tip)
- 6 drops lemon essential oil
- 1–2 drops red food coloring (optional)
- ½ cup superfine/castor sugar
- Silicone molds
- Waxed paper
- Storage container

What to Do:

1. Place the coconut oil, shea butter, and beeswax in a small microwave-safe bowl or container. Microwave at high power for 30-second stretches, stirring periodically with a chopstick or craft stick as oils begin to melt. When all the oils have mostly melted, remove from the microwave and stir to complete the melting and to combine.
2. Stir in the essential oils and food coloring (if using).

3. Slowly pour in the sugar while stirring. If the mixture gets stiff, pop it in the microwave for 15–20 seconds.
4. Pour or scoop the mixture into the silicone molds and set aside to cool. Half an hour in the freezer should do it.
5. Wrap the bars individually in waxed paper, then store them in a sealed container. If your climate is hot and you find your scrub bars getting a bit mushy or melty, pop them in the fridge.
6. To use the scrub bar, warm it between your hands a bit, then gently rub it against your skin to lightly buff away dead skin cells. Follow with a warm-water rinse. Alternatively, take a bar into the shower or bath with you. (Use smaller portions for this, as the scrub bars will melt in the warm water!)

Tip:

+ Pure rose essential oil is extremely expensive. Bottles of rose essential oil usually come already diluted; using that kind is absolutely fine. You may want to adjust the amount of rose oil up or down according to your sensitivity. For extra rose power or to replace some of the essential-oil blend, you can crumble a few dried rose petals into the blend as you're mixing it all together.

Lemon Rosemary Salt Exfoliating Scrub

Scrub bars are easier to handle to exfoliate your body in the bath, but for feet and hands, you may prefer a loose scrub. This is a bright, citrus and herbal–scented scrub that will lift your spirits while polishing away dead skin. Lemon is excellent at removing negative energy and encouraging joy, while rosemary is good for healing, protection, and improving focus.

What You Need:

- 1 cup salt
- Juice of 1 medium lemon
- Zest of 1 medium lemon
- 1½ tablespoons olive oil
- 1 sprig fresh rosemary
- 8-ounce glass jar with lid

What to Do:

1. Mix the salt and the lemon juice. Stir in the lemon zest.
2. Stir in the olive oil and mix thoroughly. (Add more if you want your scrub to be less dry.)
3. Chop the rosemary sprig finely and add to the mixture. If you don't want the woodier stems, strip the leaves off and discard the stems, chopping the leaves alone.
4. Store in a small jar. Allow to mellow for a day or so; stir or shake before using. Keep scrub in the fridge or another cool spot because of the fresh rosemary.
5. To use, scoop out some of the scrub and massage it gently on your skin. Rinse with warm water and pat dry.

Tip:

- Try to use finely ground sea salt for this one. The coarser the salt, the harsher the scrub will be on your skin.

Vanilla Cookie Sugar Scrub

This scrub has a cozy, comforting smell. If you're a fan of freshly baked cookies, this may be the scrub for you! Coconut oil has a subtle fragrance and feels luxurious on the skin. This recipe is so good it smells like dessert. (Technically it's not, although all the scrub ingredients are safe for consumption. If you lick your fingers, I won't tell.)

What You Need:

- ¼ cup coconut oil
- ¼ cup brown sugar
- ¼ teaspoon vanilla extract
- 4-ounce glass jar or plastic storage container with lid

What to Do:

1. Mix all the ingredients together in a small jar.
2. To use, massage onto skin, then rinse with warm water. Pat dry.

Tip:

- Wouldn't this smell amazing with a pinch of ground cinnamon? Then it could be a Snickerdoodle Scrub. Or add a pinch of ginger, nutmeg, cinnamon, and allspice and make a Gingerbread Scrub!

Bath Bombs: Master Recipe

These delightful little fizzies are excellent magical tools. Visualize the bubbles filling you with the energy you've programmed into the bath bomb, or imagine the fizziness scouring away negativity. The yield of the recipe depends on the size of your molds, but if each bath bomb is about ¼ cup, then it should make about 18. If your mold is a bit bigger or smaller, your yield will be different. Citric acid can be found in health food stores, in wine-making shops, or ordered online.

This is the basic recipe and instructions. Following it are various magical versions you can make. Use them as inspiration and design your own!

What You Need:

- Small glass or plastic bowl
- 1½ cups baking soda
- ¼ cup Epsom salts
- ¾ cup cornstarch
- Food coloring
- 1–2 teaspoons water
- Plastic gloves
- Essential oil(s) of your choice (or see recipes that follow)
- ¾ cup citric acid
- Silicone or plastic molds (see tip)

What to Do:

1. In a glass or plastic bowl, whisk together the baking soda, Epsom salts, and cornstarch.
2. Add a couple of drops of food coloring in a color you associate with your magical goal (see following recipes) to the water. Add it a few drops at a time to the dry mixture and mix well with gloved hands. Don't add too much water at once; your goal is to avoid activating the fizz of the baking soda. When the mixture holds its shape when you press some of it together, add between 6–8 drops of essential oil and mix well. Mix in the citric acid.

3. Firmly pack scoops of the blend into each mold. Don't fuss too much about how pretty it looks; just press it in firmly. Allow it to set 2–3 hours, then gently pop the shapes out and let them dry out for another day. Store them in an airtight container.

4. Repeat until the base mixture has all been molded.

Tip:

• Soap molds and large candy molds work well for this craft. Silicone muffin tins are great, too, because you can also use them to make the scrub bars in this chapter. Make sure to reserve molds used for body-care products for that use only.

Moon Magic Bath Bombs

This bath bomb is full of lunar energy to help you open yourself to intuition, serenity, and the acceptance of flow and transition. This will make roughly 4 bath bombs of approximately ¼ cup each; adjust your number of stones if your molds use more or less than ¼ cup each.

What You Need:

• 8 tablespoons baking soda
• 1½ tablespoons Epsom salts
• 3 tablespoons cornstarch
• ¼–½ teaspoon water
• ½ teaspoon freshly grated lemon zest
• ½ teaspoon crumbled dried rose petals
• Blue or purple (or blue and red) food coloring
• 4 drops jasmine essential oil
• 4 drops lemon essential oil
• Silicone or plastic molds
• 4 small moonstones

What to Do:

1. Center and ground.
2. Follow the general instructions for the previous Bath Bombs: Master Recipe. Add the zest and petals while blending the ingredients together, saying, *"Lemon, bring me joy; rose, bring me love of myself."*
3. Add a few drops of the blue food coloring to the water to tint the mixture a very pale blue. If you want a pale lavender but don't have purple, use part blue and part red.
4. Add the essential oils and say, *"Jasmine, lend your serenity; lemon, bring me purification."*
5. Pack ⅛ cup of the mixture into a mold, place the moonstone in the center, then pack the second ⅛ cup on top. Press down firmly. Repeat with the next three molds.

Tiger Magic Bath Bombs

This bath bomb is designed for courage and strength to help you boost your confidence. This will make roughly 4 bath bombs of approximately ¼ cup each; adjust your number of stones if your molds use more or less than ¼ cup each.

What You Need:

- 8 tablespoons baking soda
- 1½ tablespoons Epsom salts
- 3 tablespoons cornstarch
- ¼–½ teaspoon water
- 1 pinch ground ginger
- 1 pinch ground nutmeg
- Yellow or orange (or yellow and red) food coloring
- 4 drops bergamot essential oil
- 4 drops sandalwood essential oil
- Silicone or plastic molds
- 4 small tiger's eye stones

What to Do:

1. Center and ground.
2. Follow the general instructions for the Bath Bombs: Master Recipe. Add the spices while blending the dry ingredients together, saying, "*Ginger, bring me power; nutmeg, bring me courage.*"
3. Add a few drops of the food coloring to the water to tint the mixture yellow or orange. If you don't have orange, use part yellow and part red.
4. Add the essential oils and say, "*Bergamot, lend me your positivity; sandalwood, bring me grounding and confidence.*"
5. Pack ⅛ cup of the mixture into a mold, place a tiger's eye stone in the center, then pack the second ⅛ cup on top. Press down firmly. Repeat with the next three molds.

Blessing Bath Bomb

If you feel like you need a bath that purifies and uplifts you, look no further. This magical bath bomb will do the trick. This will make roughly 4 bath bombs of approximately ¼ cup each; adjust your number of stones if your molds use more or less than ¼ cup each.

What You Need:

- 8 tablespoons baking soda
- 1½ tablespoons Epsom salts
- 3 tablespoons cornstarch
- ¼–½ teaspoon water
- ½ teaspoon crumbled dried rose petals
- ¼ teaspoon silver biodegradable cosmetic-grade glitter (optional)
- 4 drops jasmine essential oil
- 4 drops sandalwood essential oil
- Silicone or plastic molds
- 4 small clear quartz stones

What to Do:

1. Center and ground.
2. Follow the general instructions for the Bath Bombs: Master Recipe. Add the petals while blending the dry ingredients together, saying, "*Rose, bring me purification.*"
3. Blend the glitter, if using, into the dry mixture.
4. Add the essential oils and say, "*Jasmine, uplift me; sandalwood, bless me.*"
5. Pack ⅛ cup of the mixture into a mold, place a clear quartz stone in the center, then pack the second ⅛ cup on top. Press down firmly. Repeat with the next three molds.

Tip:

♦ Cosmetic-grade glitter is fun to add to this bath bomb.
Remember, less is more (no more than ¼ teaspoon per smaller
recipe batch), and wipe down your tub after using it if you have
pets! Look for biodegradable glitters.

Gentle Dreams Bath Bomb

Remove negativity and soothe your stress before bed by using this
bath bomb full of lavender and lemon balm.

What You Need:

♦ 8 tablespoons baking soda
♦ 1½ tablespoons Epsom
  salts
♦ 3 tablespoons cornstarch
♦ ¼–½ teaspoon water
♦ 1 teaspoon ground dried
  lavender
♦ 1 teaspoon dried lemon
  balm

♦ Lavender (or blue and
  red) or blue food coloring
♦ 4 drops lavender essential
  oil
♦ 4 drops ylang-ylang
  essential oil
♦ Silicone or plastic
  molds

What to Do:

1. Center and ground.
2. Follow the general instructions for Bath Bombs: Master Recipe.
   Add herbs while blending the dry ingredients together, saying,
   "Lavender, bring me peace; lemon balm, bring me sleep."
3. Add a few drops of the food coloring to the water to tint the
   mixture pale lavender or pale blue.
4. When you add the essential oils, say, *"Lavender, lend me your
   relaxation; ylang-ylang, bring me calm."*

5. Firmly pack the blend into the molds. Allow it to set 2–3 hours, then gently pop the shapes out and let them dry out for another day. Store them in an airtight container.

Bath Oil

Bath oil is a simple, luxurious addition to your bath that is very easy to make. Here's the basic recipe to adapt as you like, followed by specific magical recipes. Good carrier oils to choose for this project are jojoba oil, grapeseed oil, or sweet almond oil, most of which can be found at your grocery or health food store.

What You Need:

- Bottle with lid
- 1 cup carrier oil of your choice
- 8–10 drops of essential oil (your choice, or see following recipes)
- Label and pen or marker

What to Do:

1. Pour the carrier oil into the bottle. Add the essential oils. Cap the bottle and gently shake to blend the oils. Clearly label the bottle with the contents and the date the oil was blended. Allow the oil to rest at least a week, if possible, to develop before using.
2. To use, add 2–4 tablespoons to your bath and swish your hands around to help disperse the oil in the water. Be cautious as it can make the tub slippery.

Relaxing Bath Oil

This is a lovely, all-purpose blend for relaxing in the bath. It's good before bed, or when you need to unwind after a tense day at work. Make sure the stone is small enough to fit in the bottle you intend to use.

What You Need:

- Rose quartz stone
- 1 cup carrier oil
- Bottle with lid
- 5 drops lavender essential oil
- 3 drops frankincense essential oil
- 2 drops sandalwood essential oil
- White candle and candleholder
- Matches or lighter
- Label and pen or marker

What to Do:

1. Cleanse the stone as per your preferred method (see Chapter 1).
2. Pour the carrier oil into the bottle. Add the essential oils. Cap the bottle and gently shake to blend the oils.
3. When the oil has been shaken, add the stone to the bottle. Place the bottle in front of the candle. Light the candle and say, "*Bless this oil, that I may release tension and stress when I use it.*"
4. Let the candle burn down. Label the bottle.
5. Allow the oil to rest at least a week, if possible, to develop before using.
6. To use, add 2–4 tablespoons to your bath and swish your hands around to help disperse the oil in the water.

Joyful Bath Oil

This bath oil is just the thing to lift your spirits and refresh your optimism!

What You Need:

- Citrine stone
- 1 cup carrier oil
- Bottle with lid
- 5 drops lemon essential oil
- 3 drops frankincense essential oil
- 2 drops sweet orange essential oil
- Yellow candle and candleholder
- Matches or lighter

What to Do:

1. Cleanse the stone as per your preferred method (see Chapter 1).
2. Pour the carrier oil into the bottle. Add the essential oils. Cap the bottle and gently shake to blend the oils.
3. When the oil has been shaken, add the stone to the bottle. Place the bottle in front of the candle. Light the candle and say, "*Bless this oil, that it may bring joy and happiness whenever I use it.*"
4. Let the candle burn down. Label the bottle.
5. Allow the oil to rest at least a week, if possible, to develop before using.
6. To use, add 2–4 tablespoons to your bath and swish your hands around to help disperse the oil in the water.

Bath Salts

Epsom salts are used to soothe achy muscles and can help reduce inflammation. This recipe may seem like it makes a lot, but if you use 2 cups per bath, then it goes quickly! Make sure to soak at least 15 minutes to get the benefit from the salt. This recipe makes about 5 cups; you can divide it and add different colors and scents to different bottles, if you choose.

What You Need:

- 3 cups coarse sea salt
- 1½ cups Epsom salts
- ½ cup baking soda
- Medium bowl
- 12–16 drops essential oils
- Containers or jars with lids

What to Do:

1. Mix the dry ingredients in the bowl.
2. Add essential oils a few drops at a time and mix thoroughly.
3. Store the bath salts in sealed containers to keep out moisture.
4. To use, pour 1–2 cups into the bath while the water is running.

"Serenity Now" Bath Salts

Salts are great for relaxing overworked muscles. The herbs and oils in these bath salts are great for an overworked mind and spirit. Who doesn't need some serenity after a long week? This recipe makes about 2½ cups.

What You Need:

- Amethyst stone
- 1½ cups coarse sea salt
- ¾ cup Epsom salts
- ¼ cup baking soda
- Medium bowl
- 2 tablespoons dried lavender flowers
- 2 tablespoons dried rose petals, crumbled
- 8 drops lavender essential oil
- 6 drops jasmine essential oil
- Glass jar with lid

What to Do:

1. Cleanse the amethyst according to your preferred method (see Chapter 1).
2. Mix the salts and baking soda in a medium bowl. Add the dried flowers and combine.
3. Add essential oils a few drops at a time and mix thoroughly.
4. Place the amethyst in the bottom of the jar. Pour the bath salts in on top of it and cap the jar.
5. Center and ground. Hold the jar in your hands and draw energy up from the earth to your core, then down your arms to the jar in your hands. Visualize it sparkling with energy. When you feel it has been charged adequately, stop. Put it down and allow the energy you've been drawing up to sink back into the earth. Shake your hands to rid them of any excess energy.
6. To use, pour 1–2 cups of bath salts into the bath while the water is running.

Milk Bath Powder

Milk has lactic acid, which works to soften the skin by encouraging dead skin cells to slough off. Cornstarch helps soothe and relieve dry, itchy skin. Magically, milk is associated with nourishment, longevity, and healing energy. Salt possesses purifying and protective energy. The optional oat flour makes the bath even silkier and soothing to the skin. This recipe makes enough for three baths.

What You Need:

- 1½ cups whole-milk powder
- ½ cup Epsom salts
- ½ cup cornstarch
- ½ cup baking soda
- ½ cup oat flour (optional)
- Medium bowl
- 10 drops essential oil(s) of your choice
- 4-cup glass jar with lid
- Label and pen or marker

What to Do:

1. Stir the dry ingredients together in the bowl. Add the essential oil(s) and stir thoroughly.
2. Store in a glass jar with a lid, and label with the blend and date you made it.
3. To use, scoop out 1 cup of the powder and pour it into the bath. Swish your hand through the water to help disperse and dissolve the blend.

Tip:

- If you're lactose intolerant, you can use powdered goat's milk. If you're vegan, use soy milk, coconut milk, or rice milk; they won't have the same physical effects that lactic acid has, but they'll still feel luxurious, and all of them carry the magical associations of protection and health. If you can't get your preferred milk powdered, mix the oils with the liquid milk, then add the rest of the ingredients and stir to combine. If you use a liquid milk, store the blend in the fridge and shake to blend again before you use it in the bath.

Lavender Mint Milk Bath

Lavender is soothing and good for gentle purification. Mint is another good purifier and also supports good health and success.

What You Need:

- 1½ cups whole-milk powder
- ½ cup Epsom salts
- ½ cup cornstarch
- ½ cup baking soda
- ½ cup oat flour (optional)
- Medium bowl

- 10 drops essential oil(s) of your choice
- 1 tablespoon dried lavender flowers, roughly ground
- 1 tablespoon dried mint, crumbled
- 3½-cup glass jar with lid
- Label and pen or marker

What to Do:

1. Stir the dry ingredients together in the bowl. Add the essential oil(s) and stir thoroughly.
2. Stir the lavender and mint into the blend. Hold your hands over the jar and say, *"Powers of lavender and mint, bless this bath with health, peace, and purification. So may it be."*
3. Store in a glass jar with a lid, and label with the blend and date you made it.
4. To use, scoop out 1 cup of the powder and pour it into the bath. Swish your hand through the water to help disperse and dissolve the blend.

Honey Milk Bath

Honey is associated with immortality, healing, happiness, beauty, and abundance. Honey is soothing and nourishing for the skin. Almonds are also associated with abundance as well as wisdom and healing. Chamomile resonates with healing and peaceful energy, and lavender is used for peace and purification. For extra luxury, gently massage honey onto your face as a mask while you soak in this Honey Milk Bath. Wash it off with warm water and a gentle circular motion after your bath.

What You Need:

- 1½ cups whole-milk powder
- ½ cup Epsom salts
- ½ cup cornstarch
- ½ cup baking soda
- ½ cup oat flour (optional)
- Medium bowl
- 10 drops essential oil(s) of your choice
- 2 teaspoons sweet almond oil
- 1 teaspoon honey powder or crystals
- 1 teaspoon dried rose petals, ground to powder
- 1 teaspoon dried lavender flowers, ground to powder
- 4-cup glass jar with lid
- Label and pen or marker

What to Do:

1. Stir the dry ingredients together in the bowl. Add the essential oil(s) and stir thoroughly.
2. Stir in the almond oil, honey powder, rose petals, and lavender flowers.
3. Center and ground. Hold the jar in your hands or your hands over the bowl and say, "*I call on the energy of honey, almond, rose, and lavender to bring me peace and healing. So may it be.*"

4. Store in a glass jar with a lid, and label with the blend and date you made it.
5. To use, scoop out 1 cup of the powder and pour it into the bath. Swish your hand through the water to help disperse and dissolve the blend.

Skin Care

Part of basic self-care is making sure you hit the necessities: food, hygiene, sleep, and so forth. Sometimes you shortchange your body, often because you're uncomfortable within it. One way to become more comfortable in your body is to pay it more attention, to honor and respect it. Making this lovely Body Butter to moisturize your skin is a way of showing yourself a bit of love.

Body Butter

Drinking enough water to hydrate your body from the inside is a goal you should always have. This silky, luxurious Body Butter is a lovely way to treat yourself to well-nourished skin from the outside as well. Make sure you allow the melted mixture to cool; this is what allows you to whip it into lovely, fluffy, silky butter. Makes approximately 1 cup.

What You Need:

- ¼ cup shea butter
- ¼ cup cocoa butter
- ¼ cup coconut oil (solid)
- Glass bowl
- Medium saucepan ⅓ full of water
- Wooden chopstick or craft stick
- ¼ cup sweet almond oil
- 10 drops essential oil(s) of your choice (optional)
- Hand mixer
- 8-ounce glass jar with lid

What to Do:

1. Place the butters and the coconut oil together in the glass bowl.
2. Set the glass bowl on top of the saucepan and warm the saucepan over medium-low heat until the water is simmering. Stir the butters and oils periodically with the wooden stick until they have melted. Remove from heat.
3. Stir in the sweet almond oil.
4. Place the bowl in the fridge about 1 hour, then check to see if the mixture has turned opaque. Look for a texture like soft wax forming. If the mixture has solidified too much, just leave it on the counter for a while to warm up.
5. Remove the bowl from the fridge and add the essential oils, if using. With the hand mixer, start beating the cooled mixture and continue until it's light and fluffy, the mixture has lightened in color, and the whipped mixture holds its shape on the mixer beaters.
6. Spoon the whipped butter into a glass jar, cap it, and write the name and date on it somewhere.
7. To use, take a dab on your finger and rub it into your skin. A little goes a long way. The Body Butter may feel greasy at first, but it will absorb quickly.
8. If the butter hardens, remelt it with a bit more sweet almond oil, then repeat the cooling and whipping process.

Tip:

+ You can use other butters or oils when making this. Just remember to substitute solids for solids and liquids for liquids! Also, shea butter can have a very strong scent if it's unrefined. If it's too much for you, you have a few options: look for refined shea butter instead; decrease the shea butter to ⅛ cup and up the cocoa butter by ⅛ cup; or use another butter like mango or kokum butter in place of the shea butter. You can also substitute other light oils for the sweet almond oil, such as jojoba, hemp, sunflower, or grapeseed oil.

Magical Body Butter Blend: Serenity

This Magical Body Butter Blend uses the soothing energies of jasmine, rose, and ylang-ylang to create a blend that attracts balance and peace. The pale blue candle and amethyst, jade, and moonstone used to bless it also work to underline peace and to calm stress.

What You Need:

+ 1 recipe Body Butter (see recipe in this chapter)
+ 4 drops jasmine essential oil
+ 4 drops rose essential oil
+ 2 drops lavender essential oil
+ Pale blue candle and candleholder
+ Matches or lighter
+ Amethyst stone
+ Jade stone
+ Moonstone

What to Do:

1. Prepare the Body Butter as per the previous recipe, adding the jasmine, rose, and lavender oils where essential oils are indicated in the recipe.

2. When the Magical Body Butter is finished and placed in the container, bring it to your work space. Set the candle in the center of the work space, place the container of butter in front of it, and arrange the three stones in a semicircle in front of the container.

3. Light the pale blue candle, and say:

    Spirits of serenity,
    I invite you here.
    Lend to this butter your peace, your calm.
    May I be blessed by you each time I use it.

4. Touch the amethyst and say, "*Amethyst, I invoke your calm. Lend it to this butter.*"

5. Touch the jade and say, "*Jade, I invoke your tranquility. Lend it to this butter.*"

6. Touch the moonstone and say, "*Moonstone, I invoke your peace. Lend it to this butter.*"

7. Sit at your work space with your eyes closed, breathing deeply, sensing the calm around you. When you feel it is right, you may extinguish the candle and leave, or allow the candle to burn down completely to continue to charge the butter.

Restful Sleep

One of the keys to reducing stress and taking good care of your body is getting adequate sleep. Easier said than done! Your mind can keep you awake long after lights out, sabotaging restful sleep, or keeping you from reaching a deep enough sleep for it to be properly restorative.

Maximizing your sleep benefit can lower blood pressure, regulate your appetite, and improve concentration and productivity. A reliable bedtime routine can help your mind settle into the proper wind-down for an easier time falling asleep. Here's a list of simple sleep-associated tips:

- Eat a light supper beforehand.
- Wash your face and remember to moisturize.
- Take a moment or so to reflect on your day, writing in your self-care journal, if you like. (See the End-of-Day Ritual in Chapter 4.)
- Put away your phone and tablet at least half an hour before lights out. If you want to read, choose a paper book. It engages the brain in a different way.
- Make your room calm, and make sure you have fresh sheets regularly. Vacuum your bedroom and tidy your flat surfaces to create as unchaotic an atmosphere as you can. (For more on care of your household, see Chapter 5.)

Also see the Bedtime Prayer exercise in Chapter 4 for another idea on how to approach bedtime.

Naps and Alternatives

As with many other self-care tips, recommending naps often assumes you have the time and space in which to have them. There is a lot of discussion about how a nap can actually make you more productive, how a brief snooze can revive you and help with mental clarity.

Well, it doesn't always work. If you struggle with anxiety or sleep problems, trying to nap can be excruciating. Fortunately, there are alternatives. Recent research has shown that even lying down for 20 minutes can have similar benefits to an actual nap, which is excellent news for those who have trouble falling asleep.

There are also times when a nap can be detrimental. If you are practicing strict sleep hygiene, naps are a bad thing because they can upset your body's rhythm to a point where your night will be out of whack again, and it can take days to recover. So what to do instead of napping?

- Meditation. Try one of the breathing meditation exercises or a mindfulness meditation from Chapter 4.
- Light exercise. Yes, it may be a drag getting yourself up and going, but a brief walk outside can clear your head and lift your mood. Part of it is the change in surroundings and the fresh air, but part of it is getting blood flowing through your muscles and breathing more deeply than you would when sitting home.

One way you can amp up your physical self-care is by boosting the quality of the sleep you get. Balms and room or linen sprays are a way to use the power of essential oils to help you relax and create an atmosphere to optimize your sleep.

Sleep Balm

Sleep balm can be rubbed on inner wrists, temples, inner elbows, and anywhere else you like. (It's especially nice on rough feet!) The oils in it support relaxation and help calm a busy mind, allowing you to fall asleep more easily.

What You Need:

- Small saucepan ½ full of water
- 2 tablespoons olive oil
- 1 tablespoon coconut oil (solid)
- 1 tablespoon beeswax (grated or pellets)
- Clean glass jar, approximately 6 ounces
- Wooden chopstick or craft stick
- 10 drops lavender essential oil
- 10 drops chamomile essential oil
- 5 drops bergamot essential oil
- 3 drops sweet orange essential oil
- 2 drops ylang-ylang essential oil
- Storage jar or container, approximately 2 ounces (or two 1-ounce containers); glass recommended

What to Do:

1. Place the saucepan on a stove burner and bring the water to a simmer over medium-low heat.
2. Place the olive and coconut oils and the beeswax in the glass jar. Place the glass jar in the simmering water to allow the contents to melt together. Use the chopstick or craft stick to stir them, or gently hold the rim of the jar and swirl the contents to help them melt and combine.
3. When the beeswax has melted and combined with the oils, turn off the burner and remove the jar from the pan.

4. Add the essential oils and swirl to combine.

5. Open your storage container(s). Carefully pour the liquid balm into them, using paper towel to wipe off the edge of the container if necessary.

6. Leave the containers to cool and the balm to solidify. The shallower your containers, the more quickly this will happen.

7. Cover the containers and store in a cool, dry place. This sleep balm will keep for about six months.

Sleep Mist

This blend of oils is designed to be sprayed with a mister over your bed. Do it about 10 minutes before you plan to get into bed, so that the sheets don't feel damp.

What You Need:

- Spray bottle
- 1 cup distilled water
- 30 drops lavender essential oil
- 10 drops chamomile essential oil
- 8 drops ylang-ylang essential oil

What to Do:

1. Nearly fill the spray bottle with the distilled water.

2. Add the essential oils and cap the bottle. Swirl gently to combine.

3. To use it, fold back your covers. Shake the bottle gently to recombine the solution. Spray the sheets with the Sleep Mist, but don't saturate them; just let the mist settle on the fabric. Wait a few minutes for the sheets to dry a bit—you could do your bedtime routine—and then get in. Enjoy the calming scent of the oils.

Chapter 4

Spiritual Self-Care

Spiritual self-care is the process of nurturing our search for meaning in life, usually by interacting with some form of power or energy greater than our own. While many recognize that spirituality is an aspect of their lives, not as many people understand that their spiritual life and relationship with the Divine or whatever they hold sacred needs tending, just as relationships between people do. This chapter explores methods through which you can engage in spiritual self-care, exploring creativity, celebration of the Divine, and your connection to the elements around you.

Spiritual Self-Care

Your spiritual life is also a source of self-care. Touching the Divine, communing with the universe at large, can be a very comforting thing that refills your metaphorical cup. It can soothe, energize, inspire, and uplift you, depending on what you need…or what the universe thinks you need.

If you participate in an organized religion, you likely have the kind of spiritual support that naturally comes with a group of people who meet regularly and follow a prescribed set of rituals within the context of a particular calendar. If you follow a personal spiritual path, however, where your spirituality evolves based on your individual experiences with the Divine, then you carry a lot more responsibility for the direction your spirituality takes. This kind of spiritual path depends on frequent reflection and listening to intuition in order to keep it functioning in a fulfilling way.

Spirituality should be joyful and celebratory. If you're feeling like something's lacking, something's not quite fitting right, or you're miserable within your spiritual practice, then you're doing something wrong and definitely need to reevaluate your spiritual practice in order to make it as rewarding as possible.

Gods

If you follow a nature-based alternative spiritual path, chances are good you might consider your path as being under the pagan (or neo-pagan) umbrella. While you don't have to be pagan to practice magic, a large number of magic practitioners do self-identify as pagan, and that's what this section is about.

Do you identify as a follower of a monotheistic religion, or an established alternative path with clearly specified deity or deities associated with it, or perhaps powerful entities such as saints, bodhisattvas, or angels? Go ahead and call on them to bless and/or lend support to your work.

A relationship with some aspect of the Divine, be it a specific godform or an abstract, can be deeply rewarding. Putting a face or name to the magical, divine power that animates the universe can be very therapeutic and make your relationship with the universe at large much easier.

Worship is part of it, but it isn't self-subjugation; it's a joyful celebration of the deity. It's celebrating the rich, complex relationship you can develop with a deity via communication, meditation, aligning yourself with the deity's values and associated areas of power.

A relationship with a deity isn't very different from relationships with other human beings or sentient creatures. It takes time, attention, and awareness. And like the more familiar kind of relationships, sometimes we're swept away by an instant connection, but sometimes it takes a while to really get to know someone.

It's important to know that a relationship with a deity may not last a lifetime. There may come a time when your connection to a specific deity fades and they release you. There may be a new deity that it is time for you to work with. The trick is making sure that the relationship has proper closure and is not just wilting from a lack of effort on your part.

If you feel called by deities or drawn to them in some way, but you feel uncomfortable with them, it is perfectly all right to thank them and say no, politely and respectfully. Try researching associated deities or similar deities from other cultures. You may find a parallel deity clicks for you.

Getting to know deities can be done through meditation, reading about them, or familiarizing yourself with their areas of association. For example, is the deity you're drawn to a harvest deity? Try working with a garden for a while! Or you might wish to work on a project or craft that honors them. In general, just talk to them. Try adding a brief prayer in the morning or evening to acknowledge their presence in your life (as simple as "Bright Lord, help me get through my day with a smile" or "Lady of the Moon, thank you for my many blessings this day").

Aside from sources of natural energy people draw on in magic (such as crystals and stones, flowers and herbs, elemental energies, and more), one source of energy people often draw upon is that of deities, or some form of the Divine. This brings folk magic into the realm of religious magic. You don't have to practice one or the other exclusively.

Working with divine energy is not like plugging something into an equation, however. It's dependent on your personal relationship with the deity in question. It would be rude to invoke a deity to lend their aid to a spell or ritual if you'd never bothered to introduce yourself or cultivate some sort of relationship between the two of you, wouldn't it? A relationship with a deity should always be founded on deep respect.

If you work with generic godforms, such as God and Goddess or Lord and Lady, you might have a bit more leeway. Generic godforms are often seen as all-encompassing, containing multitudes of various expressions of the male or female aspect of the Divine. It's polite to declare yourself to the godforms, and a personal relationship is encouraged. If you are considering working or invoking a particular deity, etiquette calls for a specific introduction at the barest minimum before invoking them (remember, respect is the foundation of a good relationship). Research the deity and find out about its culture or origin, what its likes and dislikes are, what its areas of association are in order to become as familiar with them as possible.

For self-care magic, read up on deities associated with such areas as hearth and home, health management, and protection. Here are some examples:

- Apollo (Greek): healing, enlightenment, reason
- Brigid (Celtic): hearth, healing

- Demeter (Greek): abundance, cycles, household
- Durga (Hindu): protection, strength
- Eir (Norse): healing
- Frigga (Norse): hearth and household, protection
- Idunn (Norse): longevity, good health
- Isis (Egyptian): healing, protection
- Kuan Yin (Buddhist): compassion, mercy, health
- Minerva (Roman): wisdom, strategy

Animals

Animal energies can also be invoked or called on to help power spells or enhance rituals. If you have a particular animal that you feel drawn to or connected with, that may be an animal spirit that functions as a spiritual guardian for you. Sometimes you deliberately invoke a specific animal in a spell because of its magical associations with your goal, and you request that the animal lend its energy to help you because you want to learn from its energy and the lessons it can teach you. In this case, the animal is a spiritual teacher.

Like deities, it's important to know that relationships with animal spirits may not last a lifetime. There may come a time when your connection to a specific animal fades and they release you (or you release them). Thank them for their time and lessons.

Animals associated with serenity, harmony, calm, health, protection, and other areas associated with self-care include:

- Bear: conservation of energy, nurturing
- Crane: patience, healing, balance
- Deer: family, kindness, peace
- Dove: peace, calm
- Dragonfly: harmony, change
- Fox: avoiding complications, discretion, staying in background
- Hummingbird: joy, hope
- Moth: transformation
- Otter: joy, play
- Owl: wisdom, insight, honesty with yourself
- Squirrel: resourcefulness, caution, balance
- Swan: transitions, peace, spiritual evolution

Animal Invocation/Honoring Ritual

Sometimes to support your self-care, you might want to invite the spirit of a certain animal to help you out. If you are drawn to an animal that isn't generally associated with an energy related to self-care, research its behavior and habitat and life cycle. You may discover something that resonates with an aspect of self-care you're looking for.

This ritual calls for a representation. It can be a small figurine, a postcard, even a photo printed from the Internet. To further support the energy relationship you're aiming to create, you might collect other things that remind you of the animal or that depict it in some way. Consider making a little shrine somewhere, perhaps.

What You Need:

- A representation of the animal you wish to call on
- Small dish of fresh water

What to Do:

1. Center and ground.
2. Visualize the animal standing before you. Say:

    [Name of animal], I call to you.
    I ask that you lend me your energy
    That I may live a better life,
    Cared for, safe, and supported.
    In token of this request,
    I offer you this fresh water,
    Symbolic of life, transformation, and purification.
    [Animal],
    Bless me with your gifts.
    So may it be.

3. Hold the representation of the animal in your hands and visualize the animal you imagine before you flowing into the representation. Place it behind the bowl of water.
4. A day later, pour out the water (gift it to a plant!) and place the animal representation somewhere that you will see it often and be reminded of the animal's energy.

Offerings

If you're working with deities, animals, or other spirits, and asking them for aid, the concept of an exchange is important. You're not paying them for their work; an offering is a token of your appreciation. It could be a pretty rock or flower or a small cup of milk, honey, or alcohol left outside or on your work space. It might be a cookie. Burning a candle or incense in honor of whoever has helped you is also common. If you work with a specific animal a lot, perhaps donating money to a rescue organization or wildlife preserve that focuses on the animal itself or its habitat would be appropriate.

What do you do with food or drink after you've made an offering? General theory has it that the essence or energy of the offering is absorbed by the entity, and you can dispose of the physical remains the next day.

Spiritual Community

You may not belong to an established spiritual community that offers you spiritual support, no matter what your chosen path is. That's not unusual in this day and age. What you can do is find a community of like-minded individuals that support healthy self-care in other ways, who respect your spiritual path (whatever that may be) even if they don't walk it with you.

Try looking on websites like www.meetup.com, searching for local groups on *Facebook*, or joining a few different ones that each intersect with one of your interests.

Discovering Your Spiritual Beliefs

The following rituals will help you discover, define, explore, and develop your spiritual beliefs.

Spiritual Vision Board

As with the Self-Care Vision Board in Chapter 2, this activity helps you plan out and remain inspired by quotations, images, and other sources that can inform your spiritual self-care. When you create a vision board and place it in a space where you see it often, you essentially end up doing short visualization exercises throughout the day.

This Spiritual Vision Board should have a more specific focus than your general self-care board from Chapter 2. When designing the vision board, the focus should be on how you want your spiritual self-care to reflect. Your Spiritual Vision Board should motivate and inspire you to work toward the quality of spiritual life you want to be living.

Some concepts you may wish to consider when you design your Spiritual Vision Board are:

+ Nature
+ Your engagement with the earth
+ Power animals, animal spirits
+ Representations of the Divine
+ Representations of abstracts and ideals that inspire you to be the best you can be

You could use a corkboard or poster board from a craft store, or repurpose a frame that you already have by replacing the contents with blank card stock.

Again, consider whether you want this board to be permanent or an ongoing evolution that reflects how your needs for spiritual self-care change.

What You Need:

- A foundation for your board
- Pens or markers
- Blank card stock
- Photos, souvenirs, and trinkets that support or evoke your spiritual goals

- Glue, tape, or pushpins (depending on your foundation board)
- Washi tape, stickers, and so on (optional)

What to Do:

1. Gather your supplies.
2. If you like, use the journaling ritual in Chapter 1 to prepare for the activity, including the candle and incense, if you use them. Otherwise, create a pleasant ambience to work in: adjust the lighting, put on relaxing or motivational music, and so forth.
3. Design your board. Do you want space between the objects on your board, or do you want them to overlap? Also decide if you want to fill the board completely or leave space for new things as they come into importance in your spiritual life.
4. Write an affirmation or a short list of spiritual self-care statements or goals on the piece of card stock and position it on the board.
5. Arrange the photos and/or other items around the affirmation or list as you like without attaching them. When you have decided on your layout, fasten your items to the board with glue, tape, or pushpins. Use the washi tape, stickers, and so forth to further decorate the vision board.
6. Display the Spiritual Vision Board in your chosen location.

Tip:

◆ Review your Spiritual Vision Board when you review your spirituality (see later in this chapter). It can help jog your memory or help you gauge your current emotional reaction to representations of what your values or focuses were when the board was created.

Ritual to Connect to Your World

It's not just staying open to what the universe can give you that is important. It may be hard to believe, but what you can give back to the universe and the world around you is equally significant. Speak this spell somewhere you feel connected to the world around you, be it a forest, a field, a busy street… Do it wherever you feel at one with the universe.

What to Do:

1. Center and ground.
2. Say:

> *Spirit of the universe,*
> *Help me maintain my connection to the energy beyond myself.*
> *Help me remain open to the Divine in the world around me.*
> *May I be receptive to the joy and love that flows to me.*
> *May this channel stay open and free,*
> *That I may in turn share with the universe what is unique*
> *Within me.*
> *Let our dance carry on always.*
> *So may it be.*

Ritual to Review Your Spiritual Beliefs

Hanging on to outdated spiritual beliefs and practices is a waste of energy. Doing something because you've always done it means you're performing actions without mindfulness. It's healthy to examine your spiritual beliefs, values, and practices every once in a while. Doing it will help keep you focused on what is meaningful to you and help you direct your energy in the most productive, supportive ways in your pursuit of self-care.

What You Need:

- Matches or lighter
- Meditation incense (your preferred scent or blend) and censer
- White candle and candleholder
- Self-care journal and pen

What to Do:

1. Center and ground.
2. Light the incense. Light the candle, saying, *"Bless my self-reflection. May my review of my spiritual life be honest and open, and guide me in the direction that works for my highest good. May it be so."*
3. Meditate on the following questions:

   - What are your current values?
   - How do you currently feel drawn to expressing your spirituality?
   - If you work with a specific deity (or deities), do you still feel that your energy resonates with theirs?
   - Are you feeling drawn to explore new areas of spiritual expression?
   - Does the practice of certain elements of your spirituality feel perfunctory?
   - What elements of your practice are your favorites and still bring you comfort or joy in performing?

4. Make notes in your journal as you think through these questions. Note anything else you feel that isn't covered here.

5. If this is the first time you're reviewing your spiritual practice, look at your answers and meditate on them. Is there something you need to stop doing? Is there something new to incorporate? Note your plan. If this is a follow-up evaluation, look at your plan and your previous answers and plan and ask yourself how the changes have gone. What has been a success? What has been difficult but ultimately a benefit? What has been chaotic and really not helpful at all?

6. When you are done, thank the universe for its guidance and allow the candle and incense to burn out.

Tip:

♦ Use your Spiritual Vision Board (if you created one) to help you review your spirituality. Compare how you feel and what your current values are to those expressed on your Spiritual Vision Board.

Daily Rituals

Scheduling several brief moments to pause and touch base with yourself is an excellent way to stay on top of your spiritual self-care, providing yourself with plenty of opportunity to listen to your needs. The following activities can be termed rituals because they're being done with awareness and intent. Habits are things you do as a matter of course, with regularity, but done without awareness.

Do you work nights or swing shifts? These aren't necessarily morning or evening rituals; use them before you begin your daily activity, whatever time that may be.

Daily Kickoff Ritual

This ritual to start off your day offers you the chance to ground yourself and prepare yourself for coming activity. It also allows you the opportunity to attune or reaffirm your relationship with the elements. Schedule this 5-minute ritual into your morning sometime when you need a moment to pause.

Note: This activity calls for some kind of oracle set or tarot deck. It's used as an open-ended, visual, inspirational trigger. If you don't have any such set or deck, you can use a set of affirmation cards or the Jar of Inspiration from this chapter.

What You Need:
- Tarot deck or oracle deck (see previous note)
- Matches or lighter
- Incense and censer (scent of your choice)
- Candle and candleholder
- Small glass or dish of water
- Quartz crystal stone

What to Do:
1. Shuffle the deck of cards and place them on your work space before you begin.
2. Center and ground.
3. Light the incense, saying, *"I honor the element of air. Bless my day with wisdom and clear communication."*
4. Light the candle, saying, *"I honor the element of fire. Bless my day with joy and creativity."*
5. Hold your hand over the glass or dish of water, saying, *"I honor the element of water. Bless my day with serenity and healing."*
6. Touch the crystal, saying, *"I honor the element of earth. Bless my day with stability and prosperity."*

7. Take four slow breaths, visualizing breathing in each of the four elements one at a time. Say, "*I honor the spirit of the universe, the spark of life that fills all things. May I shine with positivity and communicate blessings to those around me this day.*"

8. Close your eyes and clear your mind. Select a card from the deck on your work space. You can either take the one off the top of the pile or cut the deck and take one from inside. Look at the image on it and allow associations to rise in your mind. Replace the card faceup on the top of the deck.

9. Close your eyes and center and ground again. Say, "*I carry the benediction of the elements with me today. May I walk this day protected and blessed. So may it be.*"

10. Clap your hands to end the ritual. Snuff out the candle and incense and go about your day.

Tip:

♦ If you like, before you finish your morning ritual, use your journal to make note of the card you pulled from the deck and jot down your associations or what it made you think of. At the end of the day, take a quick look in the booklet or a reference book associated with your deck and note the traditional associations of the card. What is similar? What is different?

End-of-Day Ritual

This ritual allows you an opportunity to recap the day, close the figurative door on anything you don't want to carry forward, and prepare yourself for rest.

What You Need:

- Matches or lighter
- Candle and candleholder
- Self-care journal (optional; see instructions)
- Pen (optional; see instructions)

What to Do:

1. Center and ground.
2. Light the candle, saying, *"I welcome the end of my day. May its blessings illuminate my spirit."*
3. Reflect on your day. You can do this with or without writing in your self-care journal. What were the best parts? What do you wish had gone differently? What are you grateful for?
4. Inhale slowly and deeply. As you exhale, release all the negativity from your day. Do this as many times as you feel necessary.
5. Say, *"I thank the universe for my many opportunities and the lessons I encounter. May my sleep be restful and deep."*
6. Extinguish the candle.

Praying

Prayer is a form of communication with whatever you feel is bigger than yourself. That may be the universe at large or a specific deity or an abstract such as the ideal of Truth or Peace or whatever feels right for you to address.

Prayer is not the exclusive domain of organized religion. While reciting set prayers can be a comfort, freestyling them and speaking from your heart is just as valid. Prayer can express love or gratitude, request help, call for protection, and just about anything you can think of. It's very accessible.

Here are two prayers you can incorporate into your spiritual self-care practice. Use them as is, rewrite them, or come up with something entirely your own!

Bedtime Prayer

The term *bedtime prayer* may conjure up images of children kneeling at their bedsides with stern parents or nannies overseeing their murmuring, but in self-care, it's a soft, gentle expression of gratitude. It's a way to reach out in appreciation, to connect gently before falling asleep.

You can say the following prayer in your heart or aloud, whichever works better for you. Don't worry about speaking it verbatim; consider it a guideline. Adjust and expand it as you need to.

What to Do:

1. Arrange yourself comfortably, either sitting on your bed or lying down.
2. Close your eyes. Center and ground. Take three deep breaths, exhaling slowly after each one.
3. Say:

> *This day has been blessed.*
> *I thank you, universe,*
> *For these many blessings.*
> *Thank you for keeping me safe and whole,*
> *For granting me compassion and insight.*
> *Thank you for the kindnesses I received.*
> *Grant me good dreams and restful sleep,*
> *That I may be prepared for tomorrow and continue striving to be*
> *The best person I can be.*
> *So may it be.*

Morning Prayer

Starting the day off with a prayer makes sense, especially if you like capping the day with one as well. It creates balance. A prayer in the morning is a way to formally launch your day with intention and mindfulness.

What to Do:

1. Arrange yourself comfortably, either sitting on your bed or standing.
2. Close your eyes. Center and ground. Take three deep breaths, exhaling slowly after each one.

3. Say:

> *Bless this day.*
> *May I be safe and strong.*
> *Grant me insight and healing.*
> *May I be open to the love flowing toward me*
> *And sensitive enough to know when others need my help.*
> *Grant me kindness and compassion.*
> *So may it be.*

Meditation

People often glibly say "You should meditate" when you mention that you're stressed. It's frustrating to have it prescribed. It's like being told that drinking water will make things better. Of course it will, at a basic level. But how do you approach meditation to make it valuable as self-care? And who has time to do all that anyway? Meditation can be daunting to begin because your new highlighted awareness makes you notice everything that derails you. (Hint: That's okay. No one's grading you. There's a reason people *practice* meditation: it's an ongoing thing; you don't master it then stop.) Some formal types of meditation call for specific positions and mantras, which can be hard work.

> Creating an atmosphere conducive to meditation can help. Try an incense such as cedar or lily and keep it for meditation only; that way, your mindset will click into meditation mode when you breathe in the scent.

The main goal of meditation is to improve self awareness and facilitate relaxation. It's a process, not a goal-oriented thing. And it cultivates kindness, starting with yourself. By not judging yourself or self-scolding for allowing thoughts to buzz in and out of your mind during meditation, you are accepting that you are only human. Cultivating compassion, starting with yourself, is an important element of self-care.

Here are some basic recommendations when it comes to meditation:

- Be comfortable. You can sit, but don't slouch; try to be upright. Don't choose an overly soft chair; try for a straight chair or sit cross-legged on the floor. You may also lie down, but again, not on something like a soft bed (unless it's bedtime and you're using meditation techniques to fall asleep). Try a carpet or a yoga mat. A bare wooden floor might be fine, if you fold a blanket or towel to put under your head.

- Most people find it easier if they close their eyes, because it shuts out visual distraction.

- Turn off your phone, and close the windows if you hear a lot of distracting noise like traffic or people.

- When you begin, allow yourself to check in with your body. How does it feel? Notice the sensation of your limbs against the seat or the floor, the weight of your hands on your legs or folded in your lap. Relax any muscles that you have tightened.

- If your mind drifts, it can be helpful to tell yourself *wandering* and then gently redirect yourself to your focus.

- Just 5 minutes of meditation is a good goal at first. If you have to stop earlier, don't scold yourself.

- Meditation teachers often recommend daily meditation for maximum benefit. A few times a week is a good goal.

There are different kinds of meditation. Here are some types that are easy to access and can be used for brief sessions pretty much anywhere.

Preparing for Meditation

Meditation benefits from ritual preparation. Performing a set of actions leading up to your meditation can enhance and maximize your benefit, because it will take you less time to get into the right frame of mind.

Here are some tips:

- Avoid meditating on a full stomach. You may feel relaxed, but trying to meditate may send you to sleep.
- Use a regular incense to help signal to your body that the scent indicates meditation is about to happen.
- Meditating to the same piece of music is another shortcut that helps your brain get itself into the right frame of mind.

Mindfulness Meditation

Mindfulness meditation is about keeping your awareness focused on the present moment. As self-care hinges on being able to know yourself and your needs in any moment, practicing mindfulness meditation allows you to become better acquainted with your reality, your thoughts, and your body while you appreciate the moment you're in.

Mindfulness meditation allows you to observe yourself without judging. Being mindful means being aware; there's no value placed on the thoughts that arise or the fact that thoughts are arising. They are there; they happen. That is all. Observe the thought, then let it pass without pursuing it. Return your mind to how your body feels.

The goal of this is to learn to release self-judgment. It also teaches you to release judgment of situations beyond your control. Stuck in traffic? Note the fact, and let it go. There is nothing you can do, so getting angry is a detrimental use of your energy. Getting anxious about being late and possibly garnering the anger of colleagues or your supervisor is a natural response, but with practice in mindfulness meditation, you can note that you'll probably be late and then release the anger or frustration. Mindfulness meditation can help you focus less on negative emotion or thought patterns and improve your control over emotional responses.

Mindfulness can also help you break bad habits, like getting tangled up in anxiety, pessimism, and negative self-talk.

Breathing Meditation

Breathing meditation (or breath awareness) is a form of mindfulness meditation that uses the breath as a focus. Rather than allowing thoughts to float through a quiet mind, this kind of meditation uses the regular pattern of inhalation and exhalation to give your mind something to pay attention to.

The easiest way to practice breathing meditation is to just breathe and observe it as it happens. Again, no judgment or imposed control; just breathe. If thoughts distract you, release them and return your focus to your breath.

Another common form of breathing meditation is to count during each part of the breathing process. For example, inhale for the count of two, hold for the count of three, and exhale for the count of four. (The slower exhalation helps slow your heart rate and physically calm the body. This is a great way to relax while you're trying to fall asleep.)

When you breathe, notice your body. How do the mechanics of breathing work? Do you breathe deeply from your abdomen, your belly rising and falling? Do you breathe lightly, with your chest barely moving? Can you feel your back expand when you inhale? Remember: no judgment; just observe.

Walking Meditation

This is a great technique to use outdoors. It also incorporates exercise and being in fresh air, both valuable additions to your self-care regime.

Choose a path. Before you begin, close your eyes and center and ground. Feel the ground under your feet. Note how your clothing feels against your skin. Inhale and observe how the outdoor air feels as it flows into your lungs. Exhale and release any tension in your body.

Begin to walk. Without judgment, note how your body feels as you move. Observe the things you pass; don't think about them, just note them and let them go.

The point of the exercise is to be in the moment. This allows you to work on acceptance—of the self and what goes on in your environment independent of you.

Focused Meditation

Focused meditation is a technique in which you focus on one thing and one thing only. It's the antithesis of multitasking. Multitasking may seem productive, but it's a jumbled approach that means you give less than your full attention to all the things you're doing simultaneously. It actually leads to a more fragmented sense of accomplishment and does nothing to nurture the sense of stability you need to reduce stress. You can feel more like you're frazzled from juggling so many things than from doing one at a time, taking a short break, then doing the next.

You may be familiar (unwillingly so) with your mind skittering away from what you should be working on because you don't want to expend the energy required to bite into it and get it done. When you're tired—physically or mentally—it's easier to do superficial stuff. Focused meditation helps us relearn the skill of focusing on the task at hand. It goes hand in hand with the concept of awareness of the moment, which is key to self-care. Focusing your attention on the task at hand—eating, reading, exercising—allows you to be aware of all the sensations that accompany that task and offers you the opportunity to examine how you respond to them.

Drinking a Cup of Tea: Focused Meditation

This activity has you focusing on drinking a cup of tea. It may sound easy, but drinking a cup of tea can take 5 minutes. Sitting doing only one thing for 5 minutes may be more of a challenge than you expect. You may be used to scrolling through social media on your phone while you enjoy a cup of something or listening to the news. This is all about your cup of tea. The bonus is that by practicing this kind of meditation, you can actually improve your ability to concentrate on a task.

What You Need:

+ A cup of freshly brewed tea
+ Self-care journal and pen

What to Do:

1. Center and ground.
2. Look at the cup of tea. Note the design of the cup. What color is the liquid inside? Can you see the steam rising?
3. Place your hands on the cup. How does the handle feel? Is the cup hot or warm? Is the design on the cup raised or flat?
4. Lift the cup. How heavy is it? How does the shifting liquid inside affect how you hold it as you lift it to your mouth?
5. How does the tea smell? Note the temperature of the air you breathe in with the cup close to your face.
6. Take a sip. Note how the temperature of the tea feels against your lips, your tongue, your throat as you swallow. Think about the taste of the tea.
7. Continue observing the tea while you drink it. If other thoughts arise while you're enjoying your cup of tea, acknowledge them, then return your attention to the cup of tea. Don't follow the other thoughts or feel frustrated; just notice that you're having them and return your focus to the task at hand.
8. When your cup of tea is finished, jot down in your self-care journal how you feel and record your experience with the activity.

Meditation Teas

Drinking a special tea blend before you start your meditation can help you focus. Like the previous tips, the simple act of having a cup of tea when you prepare to meditate is a helpful shortcut (especially if you use the same cup and same blend of tea each time). Apart from that, the warmth is relaxing, and the drinking of the tea can be a meditation all of its own.

As noted in Chapter 3, please research any herbs you intend to ingest in any form to make sure they aren't contraindicated in combination with any medications you are currently taking or with any physical condition you might have.

Here are some suggested tea blends for you to explore. You can use herbs and spices from your cupboard or garden or you can buy small quantities of them in an herb shop or grocery. Use commercial tea bags if that's what you've got; there's no rule against opening a peppermint tea bag and a chamomile tea bag and mixing the contents together, then using half for one cup and half for a later cup.

How to Brew

The following meditation tea blends will brew one cup of tea. The basic proportion for these blends is the given amount of ingredients to one cup of boiling water, unless otherwise specified. Allow the tea to steep for up to 5 minutes, then remove the tea from the infusion.

If you're using loose tea blends, put them in a tea infuser or tea ball. If you don't have either of these, put the ingredients in the bottom of a teapot or a cup, steep the tea, then pour the infusion through a strainer into a fresh cup. Compost the herbs when you're done.

Remember, these are guidelines. Try each blend as written first, then play with the amounts next time. Take notes in your self-care journal!

Chamomile Meditation Tea

+ 2 teaspoons dried chamomile
  A classic; simple but effective. Brew as per standard instructions. Add a spoonful of honey for an extra sweet treat. If you are allergic to ragweed, a straight chamomile tea may elicit similar symptoms; if so, don't drink pure chamomile tea very often, and try to use it in combination with other herbs.

Green Tea with Rose Meditation Tea

+ 2 teaspoons green tea
+ 1 teaspoon dried rose petals or rosebuds
  Brew as per standard instructions. Adding a pinch of something lemony, such as fresh catnip, lemon verbena, or lemon balm, enhances this tea blend nicely.

Chamomile Mint Meditation Tea

+ 1 teaspoon dried chamomile
+ 1 teaspoon dried mint
  Brew as per standard instructions. Add a drop or two of lemon juice to brighten it, if you like.

Mint Rose Meditation Tea

+ 2 teaspoons dried mint
+ 1 teaspoon dried rose petals or rosebuds
+ ½ teaspoon dried chamomile

Brew as per standard instructions. Peppermint is the most common kind of mint, but you can use any mint for this recipe. If you have fresh mint available, use about 2 tablespoons of torn leaves. You can also replace the dried roses with approximately 3 medium-sized fresh petals.

Ginger Lemon Meditation Tea

- 1 × ¼" slice fresh lemon
- 1 × ¼" slice fresh gingerroot
- ½ teaspoon lavender flowers

Quarter the slices of lemon and ginger and place in the infuser with the lavender flowers. Pour a cup of boiling water over it all, and allow to steep for 5 minutes. This makes a stimulating meditation tea, as opposed to more traditional relaxing, calming teas. If the ginger is too much, reduce it by half next time.

Meditation Incense

Incense is excellent for creating ambience and purifying a space to assist in relaxation, clarity, and mindfulness. The blends listed here are for loose incense that needs to be burned on charcoal tablets, which can be purchased at ethnic grocery shops, New Age stores, or ecclesiastical supply shops. Simply combine in a small closed glass container and shake to blend. If an ingredient is chunky (for example, dried juniper berries or dried rosemary needles), crush them in a mortar and pestle first. Don't forget to label the container.

Meditation Incense #1

- 3 parts frankincense
- 2 parts dried lavender

Meditation Incense #2

- 3 parts sandalwood
- 3 parts benzoin

Meditation Incense #3

- 2 parts sandalwood
- 1 part dried orange zest
- 1 part cinnamon

Meditation Incense #4

- 2 parts sandalwood
- 1 part dried rose petals
- 1 part myrrh
- 1 part dried jasmine

Meditation Incense #5

- 2 parts frankincense
- 2 parts dried juniper berries
- 1 part sandalwood
- 1 part cinnamon
- 3 drops patchouli oil

Meditation Incense #6

- 2 parts copal
- 1 part dried jasmine
- 1 part dried lavender

Meditation Incense #7

- 2 parts frankincense
- 1 part clove
- 1 part dried grated orange zest
- 1 part dried lavender

Meditation Incense #8

- 1 part frankincense
- 1 part dried rosemary

Prayer and Meditation Beads

Many people are familiar with the Catholic rosary, Buddhist malas, and Islamic misbaha (or tasbih). Prayer beads aren't limited to organized religions, however. Prayer is a way to communicate with the universe, or your perception of the divine spirit that animates it. It is intensely personal, and because of that there is an infinite amount of variation available to you. The prayers suggested here can be changed as you need to, so that they reflect your current and ever-evolving spirituality. You can also design new prayer beads in different patterns for different sets of prayers as you need them. If you want to make a set of prayer beads infused with intention and energy from the very start, you can make the actual beads themselves as well. (See the Making Magical Rose Beads craft later in this chapter.)

> Did you know that the modern English word *bead* comes from the Middle English *bede*, which means "prayer"?

Prayer Beads

This craft creates a set of beads you can use for prayer or meditation. This particular set associates sets of self-care affirmations with each section of the meditation beads. The meditation works with the number three, which is a blessed number in many magical traditions. The number nine is, of course, three sets of three.

When making this craft, don't use beads that are too small. You want to be able to feel them in your fingers as you pray your way along the string. Put tiny spacer beads between your major beads to separate them farther and to help make the string of prayer beads more fluid in your hands.

Note: Prayer beads aren't necessarily meant to be worn. This set won't be long enough to slip over your head.

What You Need:

- Wire cutters or scissors
- Beading wire, nylon cord, or waxed linen thread (about a .015"–.018" weight works for most beads)
- 1 large bead
- Small spacer beads (approximately 40)
- 3 medium beads (color A)
- 1 set of 9 smaller beads (color B)
- 1 set of 9 smaller beads (color C)
- 1 set of 9 smaller beads (color D)
- Pendant charm or stone with loop, hole, or bail
- Jump ring, to attach pendant
- Tweezers or needle-nose pliers
- Incense of your choice and censer
- Matches or lighter

What to Do:

1. Cleanse and purify your beads according to your preferred technique (see Chapter 1).
2. Center and ground.
3. Cut about a 24" length of your wire or thread. Make a loose temporary knot about 2" away from one end. Slip the large bead on to rest against the temporary knot. Thread a spacer bead on to rest against the large bead.
4. Slip one of the medium beads (color A) onto the wire to rest against the spacer after the large bead. Thread a spacer bead on to rest against the medium bead.

5. Begin threading the first set of 9 beads (color B) onto the wire. Slip a spacer bead on after each B bead.

6. Place another medium bead (color A) on the string, followed by another spacer.

7. String the second set of 9 beads (color C) onto the wire, placing a spacer after each bead.

8. Place another medium bead (color A) onto the wire, followed by a spacer bead.

9. String the third set of 9 beads (color D) onto the wire, placing a spacer after each bead.

10. Check your string of beads to make sure you haven't missed anything in your pattern. When you are satisfied, undo the loose temporary knot and tie the ends together with a square knot. (Don't use a granny knot; it will slip open.) Trim the ends, but leave about an inch on each. Use tweezers or needle-nose pliers to feed each end back into the beads on one side or another.

11. Use your fingers, tweezers, or the jewelry pliers to open the jump ring slightly with a gentle twisting motion. Loop it through the hole or bail of your pendant charm or stone, then over the wire between the final spacer bead and the first medium bead. Press the jump ring back together firmly.

12. Once your prayer beads are done, center and ground, then purify them by passing them through incense such as frankincense or sandalwood, and say, *"I cleanse and bless you, beads. Be for me a focus and support in my pursuit of wholeness and leading a blessed life. May it be so."*

Tips:

• A dab of clear nail polish can help secure the square knot.

• Store your prayer beads in a pretty bag or box, away from strange hands and where they could pick up unwanted energy.

How to Use the Prayer Beads

Since repeating affirmations is a magical practice, why not use your self-care journaling incense and candle to accompany this exercise? It will help signal to your psyche that this is the same sort of self-care activity.

What You Need:

- Matches or lighter
- Candle and candleholder
- Incense and censer
- Prayer Beads (see previous activity)

What to Do:

1. Center and ground.
2. Light the candle and incense.
3. Hold the string of beads in your hands and take three slow, deep breaths.
4. Start with the pendant. Hold it and say, "*I am complete in myself. I am enough. I have the power to shape and change my life.*"
5. This set of beads represents healing. At the medium bead introducing this first set, say, "*I am whole and healthy; I embrace wellness.*"
6. On each of the 9 smaller beads of this first set, say, "*I welcome healing in all areas of my life.*"
7. The second set of beads represents self-confidence. At the medium bead introducing it, say, "*I am enough. I hold within me all that I need to succeed.*"
8. On each of the 9 smaller beads of this second set, say, "*I welcome growth and opportunity.*"
9. The third set of beads represents self-love. At the medium bead introducing it, say, "*I am worthy of love, respect, and care. I deserve a good life.*"

10. On each of the 9 smaller beads of the third set, say, "*I welcome love in all areas of my life.*"

11. You have gone all the way around the string of beads, and are now back at the pendant. Repeat the affirmation that began the meditation: "*I am complete in myself. I am enough. I have the power to shape and change my life. It is so.*"

Making Magical Rose Beads

Making beads from the roses you have been given for a special occasion is a lovely way to tie that appreciation and celebration into your ongoing magical self-care practice. This craft transforms the petals of roses into beads that you can use in your prayer or meditation beads. As you use them the warmth of your hands releases the scent of the roses used to make the beads. It's a beautiful and magical experience.

One full-sized rose can have around 30 petals, which will make 1–1½ cups when dropped into a measuring cup lightly, not packed down. Half a dozen roses will yield roughly 8 cups. It may seem like a lot, but the petals will be reduced a lot, first by cooking and then drying. Depending on the size you make the beads, this will yield various numbers of beads. Remember that smaller beads will dry in less time.

Note: The colors of the roses will darken and sometimes change as they cook. Don't be alarmed.

What You Need:

- Petals of 6 roses
- Blender
- Distilled water (approximately ¼ cup per 2 cups petals)
- Large saucepan (avoid stainless steel; try to use glass or enamel)
- Wooden spoon
- Rose essential oil (optional)
- 5 metal or plastic double-pointed knitting needles (US size 1 or 2)
- Square of Styrofoam or floral foam

What to Do:

1. Place 2 cups petals in the blender and add ¼ cup water. Cover and blend. Alternate adding the petals and the water. As you add more petals, hold back on the water a bit; you want a doughy texture, and the more water you add now, the more you'll have to remove later.

2. Scrape out the blended pulp into the saucepan and heat it over medium heat, stirring with the wooden spoon. Do not let the mixture boil; just heat it to thicken it further.

3. When the pulp is the consistency of clay, remove it from the heat and allow it to cool enough to be able to knead it. If your rose clay isn't scented as much as you'd like, add a few drops of rose oil and knead it in.

4. Twist off marble-sized pieces and roll them into balls. The beads will shrink to about half their original size as they dry, so plan accordingly. Gently press a ball onto a knitting needle so that the point comes out the other side, then gently slide the bead down toward the end of the needle. Continue until you have used all the clay to make beads of your desired sizes. Allow a bit of space between the beads on the needles so that air can circulate between them properly.

5. Press one end of each needle into the Styrofoam or floral foam so they stand up, to allow the air to circulate around all surfaces of the beads.

6. Spin the beads gently every day or so or move them back and forth on the needle to make sure they don't dry to the surface of the needle itself.

7. Drying time will depend on how humid or damp your weather is, how much water is still in the clay, and how large the beads are.

8. When the beads are dry, slide them off the needles. Use them in whatever bead-based craft you like.

Tips:

♦ These flower-based beads can be made with other flowers as well. Look up the magical associations of the various flowers you have and see what you can use for specific magical purposes. You can cook different flowers together to make a multiflower clay, or cook them separately and then combine the beads on your wire as you string your new set of prayer beads.

♦ If you don't have a blender, a food processor will work. You can also grind the petals by hand in a stone mortar and pestle, but it will be time-consuming.

♦ Don't get these flower-based beads wet; they're not waterproof.

Connecting to Nature

Nature is all around us, and yet we often are oblivious to it. It's a shame, because it can support your self-care in various ways. For one thing, nature is quiet—not literally, but figuratively. Nature doesn't bombard you with arguments, videos, headlines, and deadlines. There is less stress in nature.

Nature therapy provides an easy way to lower your stress levels. It can elevate your mood, give your mind a rest, and offers the chance for movement and exercise, if you choose. Being in a natural environment allows your attention to be caught in a passive, involuntary way, as opposed to a directed, active application of attention and focus, as in work or reading. Involuntary attention uses less energy than directed attention, which is why you often return from time spent in the company of nature feeling less tired than you would have if you'd spent the same amount of time in a cinema. Both are enjoyable, but a film requires attention and focus to follow the story and to process all the elements of the narrative.

Just being present in nature can reduce your stress levels. So where do you find nature?

- If you have a backyard, you can start there. Often urban sounds can intrude, so it's not ideal, but use it if you've got it!
- City parks are a civic resource open to everyone.
- If your city or town has an arboretum or a protected natural area open to the public, schedule a visit.
- Check to see if there are local farms that host work parties or visitor days. Community-supported agriculture programs (CSAs) sometimes offer produce in return for work on the farm, which can be a terrific experience.

- Look for state or provincial parks within easy commuting distance and schedule a day to explore. Or pack a picnic and your journal and just sit and enjoy the sights and sounds.

For more ways to explore nature, check out the seasonal crafts in the Creative Self-Care section later in this chapter.

Green-Space Meditation

This meditation offers you a moment to reconnect with the magical energies of nature, even in the middle of a city. One thing that often gets dropped in modern living is interacting with the natural world. Exercising is done in indoor gyms, and interaction with the natural world can be as limited as dashing from your front door to your car on the way to work.

Taking the time to just be present and mindful in nature is a form of magical self-care that is often overlooked. You may not have access to a yard; you may feel awkward in a public green space. But take the time to try this activity. It may have benefits that outweigh the discomfort.

What You Need:

- Towel or blanket

What to Do:

1. Spread out the towel or blanket in your chosen spot. If it's winter, you can forgo the towel or blanket and use a bench, a step, or the edge of a fountain or park statue.
2. Sit or lie down. Close your eyes.
3. Center and ground.

4. Inhale deeply and exhale slowly, three times. Then say (aloud or silently),

> *Mother Nature,*
> *I honor you.*
> *I open myself to you here and now.*
> *Bless me with your loving energy.*

5. Become aware of what your sense of hearing is telling you. Listen. What do you hear?

6. Become aware of what your sense of smell is telling you. Breathe in. What do you smell?

7. Become aware of what your sense of touch is telling you. Feel. What sensations do you pick up on your skin, beneath your body?

8. Become aware of what your sense of taste is telling you. Open your mouth. What do you taste on the air?

9. Become aware of what your sense of sight is telling you. Open your eyes. What do you see around you?

10. Stay there, relaxed, for as long as you like. Journal your experience, ideally there while it is fresh in your mind, or once you have returned home.

11. Before you leave, say:

> *Mother Nature,*
> *Thank you for your many blessings.*
> *Thank you for being here with me during this meditation.*
> *May your love travel with me.*

Tips:

♦ Pack a book and/or a snack to enjoy after you do your meditation. Why waste the trip and time in your green space?

♦ If your city has a botanical garden, try this meditation in different areas of it and journal the experiences. How are they different?

Seasonal Energies

Attuning to the changing energies of nature as the seasons shift is an ideal way to engage in spiritual self-care. This way you aren't fighting the energy of the world around you, wondering why you feel restless.

We tend to think of seasons as having definite beginnings and ends, which isn't at all true. They blend from one into the other, and while on one hand this is a lovely metaphor for change in life, it can also be a source of stress. When do you put the winter boots away? What do you do when there is still a foot of snow on the ground but it's 50°F outside?

The key is to celebrate the blur, the lack of defined beginning and ending. Celebrate the shift instead. Focus on the transition itself. To flow with the transition, slowly shift over your decor and wardrobe with mindfulness.

The energy of the year shifts as the seasons change. Noticing this and allowing yourself time to consciously adjust to those shifting energies can help reduce stress. Different seasonal energies can call for different methods of self-care:

+ Self-care in winter: Think heavy blankets, cozy clothes, deep comforting smells, candles scented with spices and pine, eating richer and filling food, drinking hot or warm drinks. Watch snowfalls and have snowball fights or go ice-skating. Your outdoor time may be minimal, depending on your geographic location and the severity of the weather, but enjoy what you can in whatever way appeals to you.

+ Self-care in spring: You like to still be cozy, but not as deeply. Lighten up your self-care, both literally (lighter wraps and bedspread, foods, and drinks) and figuratively (swap heavier scented candles for lighter herbal ones, and so forth). Enjoy lighter teas and warm drinks. The weather may be more accepting of increased time spent outdoors.

♦ Self-care in summer: Reach for very light wraps of cotton or linen, and enjoy the breeze and warmth of the sun. Use sunscreen! Enjoy cool drinks, gazpacho, salads with lots of vegetables in them. Stargazing is a lovely activity.

♦ Self-care in autumn: Reach for light sweaters and covers again, wear dress boots, fingerless gloves, and looped light scarves. Wrap your hands around light, warm beverages, and return to preparing soups and stews. Enjoy the special kind of golden sunlight that belongs only to fall, and engage in outdoor activities like apple picking.

There are two different ways that seasons are marked: the calendar date, which is generally between the twentieth and twenty-second of a month, and the actual *sense* of the season arriving. There is a difference between the first day of winter and the first winter day, after all. Sometimes it may be appropriate to perform a ritual or attunement on the calendar date; other times, you may feel moved to do it earlier or later in response to an environmental cue, such as the first robin of spring or the arrival of seasonal weather.

Seasonal Attunement

When the weather is suitable, go outside into your yard or to a park. Wear the appropriate footwear and clothing!

What to Do:

1. Find somewhere that you feel comfortable. Close your eyes and take three slow, deep breaths.
2. Center and ground.
3. If you are wearing gloves or mittens, take them off. Crouch down and put your bare hands on the ground. Feel the temperature of the grass or earth.
4. Look around you. What do you see? What state are the trees in? The gardens? How would you describe the colors?
5. Journal your findings and feelings. How does this attunement feel different from your previous ones?

Tip:

◆ After doing this for more than one annual cycle, you can start comparing your observations of a spring to the previous year's spring, and that of any prior years. In this way, you can start to trace changes in your environment that you might otherwise never have noticed.

Creative Self-Care

Creative self-care absolutely falls under spiritual self-care because it helps nurture something ineffable. Spiritual balance means being in harmony with your spirit and the energy of the world at large. When you work on deepening and broadening your spiritual connection to the universe, then you'll find your creativity responding as well.

Creative self-care isn't about how unique or original your self-care methods are. It's about feeding your soul. It's what gives you joy, creates excitement, gives you a place to take risks and nurture passion again. This is the area to explore if you feel dull and uninterested and need a way to boost yourself in general. Creative self-care encourages you to give your inner self attention and an outlet and encourages a positive attitude.

Taking breaks and allowing yourself to play and explore other methods of being productive and creative without a deadline or an imposed context is a valuable way to refresh your outlook and sense of capability. It may seem counterintuitive to take a break from your to-do list to engage in something unconnected, like drawing, coloring, or knitting, but creative projects tend to use a different part of your brain, which gives the overworked parts time to breathe. Disengaging from your work can paradoxically make you more productive.

Remember, spirituality isn't religion. You can be deeply spiritual (and creative) without following a prescribed religious path.

Working to express your creativity supports your spiritual journey in turn. The two are partners. The concept of *expression* is key to both creativity and spirituality. Creative expression allows you to explore and express what is in your heart and mind, to work out how you feel; it is an outlet for emotion and an opportunity to allow your subconscious to unpack complicated issues.

Working with Your Hands

Does creative expression mean every time you doodle or arrange flowers for a centerpiece you're undergoing a deep examination of some sort of thorny, complex issue? Of course not. Sometimes it just brings pleasure to engage in something creative. And remember, self-care is about joy and pleasure. It's about being happy in yourself and being in the moment. Creative pastimes can bring you just that.

It's good to disengage by focusing on something in your hands. Crafting or fixing something is a microcosm of larger issues at work or in life. You can complete a project and feel satisfaction and a sense of accomplishment. That goes a long way to filling your need for pride in your achievements, the emotional rush of success and satisfaction at completing something. There is a sense of satisfaction associated with working with your hands that is hard to get from purely intellectual problem-solving. They are like two sides of a coin. If you've wondered about the resurgence in knitting or sewing or in painting nights, the rediscovery of purely creative handcrafts is related to the need to work with your hands and focus on a project unconnected to your daily job. Hands-on creative projects offer you the chance to disconnect from stressful daily activity.

If you work in a field where creativity is a main part of your job, you know how difficult it is to be creative all the time. It's vital that you fill your own creative well in order to be able to draw from it. Read books, bake bread, garden, look out the window, go for walks… Disengage from your main creative job in order to give your creative mind a rest and allow it to recover.

Mindful Creativity

It's pretty blithe to tell someone "You should make art" when they're looking for self-care ideas. That's because it's not particularly helpful to suggest something so vague. It's more accurate to frame it as using hands-on creative techniques to help disengage the busy mind and to aid in focusing on the moment.

> **Mindfulness helps you relax and enjoy the process of being creative, rather than focusing on a product or goal. Products and goals are fine, but they're not the whole point of the activity.**

Mindfulness, as defined earlier, is allowing yourself to be present in the moment, giving what you're doing your relaxed attention. "Making art" is one of those things that encourages mindfulness. Anything that involves using your hands to create something while disengaging you from the "hamster wheel" in your brain can qualify. Feel like working through a paint-by-numbers canvas? Want to paint something at a ceramics café? Is there a coloring book and a set of fine-tipped markers you've been eyeing? Scrapbooking? Stamp art? Photography? Go for it!

Fight Self-Censoring

One of the most important rules of creative work is to not allow negative self-talk. Sure, you can identify weak areas and work to improve them—challenging yourself is a great way to grow—but don't engage in negative self-talk. Negative self-criticism is the opposite of constructive. It's *destructive*, which undermines self-care. If you tend toward negative self-talk (*This is stupid; I'm terrible at this; What*

I create will never be any good; What is even the point if I can't do it right?), this is an area that you can use to practice countering your negativity with affirmations. Remember, nurturing your creative side is for spiritual self-care. If you are constantly down on yourself, you're strangling your spiritual self-care!

> If you are anxious or afraid of creating, your mind will do anything it can to avoid it: cleaning the fridge, checking email, washing your hair, scrubbing the bathroom floor… In other words, you'll self-sabotage your own relaxation and exploration of your creativity. If you have to, set a timer and focus on whatever creative expression you've chosen to engage in for 20 or 15 minutes without stopping.

Take a Class

Honor yourself and your need for creative self-care by taking a class and learning something new. While an actual physical class somewhere would also serve to get you out of the house for something other than work or school, it isn't always possible. Fortunately, the Internet provides innumerable course opportunities, most allowing you to pursue bite-sized lessons in a larger area on your own schedule. Websites such as *Craftsy* (www.craftsy.com) or *Skillshare* (www.skillshare.com) offer low-cost creative courses in a variety of areas—woodworking, baking, sewing, watercolor, calligraphy, fiber arts, and more. Check them out. Most ask you to create an account, even if the lessons you're interested in are free; the account allows you access to site-only features. Most of these sites run specials semifrequently, so sign up for their newsletters to keep abreast of sales.

Music

You probably already use music as part of your self-care routine. You might already have a playlist to listen to if you're having a bad day, a playlist to help you "kick ass," a relaxing playlist to listen to during a commute. You might enjoy falling asleep to relaxing music, playing an energetic album to get you into the active frame of mind to clean the house, or putting on some awesome tunes for a dance party (and if you don't indulge in random dance parties, you are missing out on a ridiculously easy and fun self-care activity)—but you may not use music mindfully.

Mindfulness asks you to focus on your current task or activity, allowing yourself to be in the moment and release the hold the past or future has on you and your emotions, giving your mind and spirit a chance to rest from spinning all those plates. We often listen to music while doing other things, which puts it in the background. Listening to music mindfully offers the opportunity to explore it—and yourself—differently.

Mindful listening can offer you a greater appreciation of music you love. Actively listening to music also provides you with the opportunity to hear or notice things in the music that you missed before. You can discover so much about your favorite music by listening to it actively.

If you already rely on music for stress reduction, then listening mindfully to the music can boost its stress-reducing qualities. Listening mindfully to music that you enjoy can have a deeper impact on relieving stress, anxiety, and depression.

Playing an Instrument

Making music is another way to reduce stress. If you suffered through enforced music lessons as a child or had been upset and stressed because you couldn't master a piece of music, you might want to argue with that idea. However, research has shown that playing an instrument can lower blood pressure, decrease heart rate, ease stress, and reduce anxiety and depression. It also reroutes your mind away from work, allowing you a mental break from using your brain for your daily job, and enforces the mindfulness action of being in the moment. As a bonus, you're doing it for yourself, not for anyone else. That's a very strong self-care statement.

If you don't already play an instrument, why not learn to play one? Ukuleles are easy to find now, as are electric keyboards if you fancy piano. You'll run into plenty of conflicting advice regarding the quality of instrument to purchase—a very poor instrument can actually impede your pursuit—so why not try renting to make sure that your chosen instrument is indeed the one for you. Look for a teacher in local online listings or posted on an old-fashioned physical bulletin board at the music store. You may be able to network with a local college or university to find a teacher for private lessons. Or try some online lessons; just read as many reviews of the set you're considering buying access to before you jump in, to make sure it's taught by an experienced teacher.

Learning a new instrument will both humble and frustrate you. But allowing yourself to be challenged, working through obstacles, and coming through the other side is a great way to bolster your self-confidence. Think of each new piece or technique as a mini project, and celebrate successfully completing each one.

Creativity Affirmations

Creative projects may make people insecure and doubt their own expression. Using affirmations to support creative self-care is an easy way to remind yourself that playing with markers and paint isn't a waste of time! Try any or all of these affirmations.

* *My work is flourishing. I am flourishing.*
* *I believe in my talents and skills.*
* *I have wonderful ideas and explore them creatively.*
* *I learn and grow from every project, and all projects are therefore successful.*

Jar of Inspiration

If you're feeling discouraged about your creative output or ability, this jar of encouraging affirmations can help. Draw one out when you feel down. Or you can draw one in the morning as part of your spiritual self-care morning routine and think about it as your day unfolds.

Choose an attractive jar for this project; there is pleasure in looking at aesthetically pleasing things. If you have a bowl or wide vase you would prefer to use, go ahead! Just make sure the opening is wide enough to reach in and grab a slip of paper, and the walls aren't too tall to stop you from taking slips from the very bottom. A pretty box would also work.

What You Need:

* Slips of blank paper
* Pen
* Small jar or other container
* Small clear quartz stone
* Small citrine stone
* Small rose quartz stone

What to Do:

1. On the slips of paper, write affirmations and supportive statements. The following are suggestions, but I encourage you to develop your own!

   * *I love the person I am becoming.*
   * *I see joy everywhere I look.*
   * *Every mistake is a learning experience.*
   * *I continue to learn and grow daily.*
   * *My work does not have to be perfect to be a success.*
   * *I only have to be better than I was before.*
   * *Small steps add up to progress.*
   * *I am confident and able.*
   * *Creative energy flows through me at all times.*
   * *Every day I am more creative.*
   * *I am resourceful and confident.*
   * *I am creative in all areas of my life.*
   * *My imagination inspires me daily.*

2. Fold each slip in half. Place each one in the jar or container.

3. Hold the clear quartz, saying, *"Quartz, I call upon your clarity and energy to energize my creative life."* Place it in the container.

4. Hold the citrine. Say, *"Citrine, I call upon your powers of communication to help me express my creativity."* Place it in the container.

5. Hold the rose quartz, and say, *"Rose quartz, I call upon your energy of transformation so that any negative energy around me is transformed to positive, supportive energy."* Place it in the container.

6. Draw out a slip of paper when you need a boost for your creative confidence. Replace it once you have read it aloud a few times. Keep the affirmation in your mind and repeat it throughout the day.

Seasonal Crafts

One way to honor the seasonal shift is by taking time to do a craft. Light a candle, burn some incense, put on appropriate music that helps you get into the headspace, and reach out for the energy of the season that approaches or has arrived to help you synchronize your own energy with it.

Seasonal Bauble Craft

Making enormous seasonal decorations or going all out and decorating your entire home for a season isn't everyone's cup of tea. Here's a smaller seasonal craft you can do annually to mark the arrival of a new season, and it won't take up a lot of room. As the years pass, you will end up with a collection of little baubles you can hang in windows or pile in a bowl. This craft is specifically designed for Yuletide, but you can adapt it for other seasons as well.

Note: If you intend to use fresh material in your baubles, you will either need to wait till the material has dried before putting the ball in storage, or remove the organic material and dispose of it. The bauble won't be airtight even when you close it, so air will circulate. Try leaving it open for a few days to get some of the humidity out before you snap it together to close it.

What You Need:

- Hollow plastic craft ball (the kind that opens into two halves; your choice of size)
- Holly
- Ivy
- Mistletoe
- Tiny pine cones
- Glitter (optional)
- Short lengths of white, red, green ribbons, 3"–5" (for inside)
- Narrow ribbon, 1'–2' (for hanging)

What to Do:

1. Open the craft ball and lay it on your work surface. Arrange the holly, ivy, mistletoe, tiny pine cones, snips of ribbon, and the glitter (if using) in one half, then close the ball and gently move it until the hanging loop is at the top. The contents will shift slightly.
2. Run narrow ribbon through the hanging loop and hang your bauble in your desired spot, or place it on a dish or in a bowl to display it.

Winter Ice Lanterns

These create magical lanterns of ice to shimmer outside. If you want to use them inside, make them smaller and place them in a bowl large enough to hold the melted water. (A silver-tone bowl in stainless steel is a good choice.)

If the outside temperature doesn't go low enough to freeze water, make room in your freezer and choose your container sizes accordingly. Make sure the containers you use are not only waterproof but will withstand freezing. Remember, water expands when it freezes.

What You Need:

- Pebbles, marbles, or other weights
- Small waterproof container
- A larger waterproof container the size of your desired ice lantern
- Water
- Tea light candles

What to Do:

1. Place some of your weights inside the small container. Set the small container inside the larger container and begin pouring water into the larger container in the space between the walls of the large and small containers.

2. Watch to see if the smaller container moves. You want it to float a bit so that there will be a sturdy layer of ice at the bottom but be held down enough to make a well for your candle to rest in. Add or remove weights to adjust the position of the inner container. Add water to the larger container to bring the water level up to where you want the height of the ice lantern to be.

3. Set the container outside or in your freezer to freeze overnight.

4. When you are ready to set up the ice lantern, bring it inside and set it in the sink to warm up a bit. Remove the weights from the inside of the smaller container, then pour warm water into the smaller container to help loosen it. Lift the inner container out. Carefully invert the larger container to slide the ice lantern out.

5. If you are planning to use the ice lantern outside, place it there and put a tea light into the middle. If you are using it inside, place it in the silver bowl, set it where you want it, and put the candle inside. Enjoy the magical effect of the fire dancing inside the ice! How long the ice lantern will last will depend on the temperature of your room.

Fall Display

There's nothing like walking through a park or woodland during autumn, when the light has that golden quality and you can smell the fallen leaves. This is a free-form craft that allows you to add and arrange things as you like.

What You Need:

- Fall leaves (select as few or as many as you like; consider the size of your vase)
- 2 light tea towels
- Waxed paper
- Iron
- Large glass vase
- Twigs and small branches of shrubs (such as dogwood, burning bush, and so on)
- Small apples
- Pine cones
- Walnuts or other unshelled mixed nuts

What to Do:

1. Collect fall leaves. Go for a variety of colors and shapes!
2. Lay a tea towel down on the surface you will be ironing on. Lay a similarly sized sheet of wax paper on top. Lay the leaves on top of that, followed by another sheet of wax paper and the second tea towel. Preheat the iron to medium-low (no steam!) and iron the stack gently to help preserve them. Allow the stack to cool, then gently peel the paper away from the leaves.
3. Assemble your supplies. Start layering the decorations in the bottom of the vase. Place some of the leaves along the outside edge of the vase as you stack.
4. As you go, start inserting the branches of shrubs in the stacked fall harvest. Place apples and pine cones around them to keep them upright and in place. Add the nuts where you like.

5. Place the arrangement near your spiritual workplace or a cozy corner, or use it as a centerpiece for a table or room.

Activities to Foster Your Creativity

Do you feel that you're not a creative person? Do you have trouble letting go and just messing about? Do you need inspiration? Here are some activities to help you explore different techniques that you can use in a spiritual context.

Vision-Board Focal Balls

Make a focal ball to represent something on your vision board, such as a goal or concept you really want to focus on for a while. Saving for a vacation to Paris? Collect a tiny Eiffel Tower, make a baguette out of play dough, find a tiny wine bottle or glass charm, and add red, white, and blue ribbons. Concentrating on expanding your creative relaxation? Fill a bauble with miniature pencils, brushes, and a tiny book. Check the miniatures area of your craft store for ideas, or make your own miniature objects out of clay. If what you want to use is too big to fit into a bauble, buy a small glass jar instead and use that.

Hang the bauble or place the jar where you will see it often. When you see it, it will bring your goal to your conscious mind and reinforce your commitment to that goal.

What You Need:

- Hollow plastic craft ball (the kind that opens into two halves; your choice of size) or a small clear-glass jar
- Trinkets, pictures, or other representations of your goal
- Adhesive gum or play dough

What to Do:

1. Open the plastic ball. In the lower half, use your trinkets and other items to build your little diorama or display, using the adhesive gum or play dough to affix things in place.
2. Gently snap the upper half onto the ball. Hang or place the ball where you can see it and be reminded of your goal.

Weaving

Weaving is a magical craft. It literally weaves disparate things together to create a useful solid piece of fabric. It is very meditative. For this craft, you can use whatever colors of yarn you want. For your first time, try to use worsted-weight yarn for the warp (the vertical lines of yarn); check the band or tag of the yarn for the weight. Worsted is a medium-weight yarn, and the band may have a yarn ball–shaped symbol with the number 4 on it. You can use thinner or thicker yarn for the weft (the back-and-forth horizontal yarn) if you like, but worsted is great for that as well. When you get to the actual weaving stage, you can use one color or several different ones and change colors where you feel like it.

This craft looks long and complicated on paper, but it just needs a lot of words to describe what to do. Read through the whole thing before starting so you know what to expect. Basically, you're creating a frame loom and you'll be weaving a tapestry on it.

Made as written, this craft will create a woven piece about 4" × 6". If you want something bigger, scale up your piece of cardboard accordingly and use more craft sticks to raise the warp all the way across your loom.

What You Need:

- Piece of cardboard about 6" × 8"
- Pencil
- Ruler
- Scissors or craft knife
- 2 standard craft sticks
- Glue
- Masking tape
- Yarn (DK to worsted weight, in colors of your choice)
- Plastic or metal weaving/tapestry needle
- Fork or wide-toothed comb
- 2 twigs (or 2 more craft sticks)

To Set Up the Loom:

1. Set your piece of cardboard in front of you, short side at the bottom so that you have a vertical rectangle.

2. With your pencil and ruler, draw a line across the cardboard ½" from the top edge.

3. Measure ½" along the line from the left edge. Make a mark. Measure ½" in from the right edge and make a mark there as well. These will be the outside edges of your woven piece.

4. Between these two marks, make 10 evenly spaced hash marks from the line up to the edge of the cardboard. (They'll be approximately ⅜" apart. Don't stress about exact measurements.)

5. Repeat steps 2, 3, and 4 along the bottom of the cardboard.

6. With the scissors or craft knife, make slices all the way through in the edges of the cardboard along the hash marks, stopping at the horizontal pencil line. Do this at the top and the bottom of the cardboard.

7. Lay a craft stick across the top of the cardboard along the pencil line so that the upper edge of the stick is at the bottom of the incisions, and glue it in place. Repeat along the bottom with the other craft stick. (These sticks will raise the warp so that you

have room to slip the needle underneath the yarn as you weave. It also reinforces the incisions, so they don't tear.)

8. While the glue dries, measure out a piece of yarn about 7' long for your warp. Use a piece of masking tape to secure one end to the reverse side of the loom at the top of the cardboard. Bring it up over the top and press it down until it catches in the first incision along the top edge. Run it down and press the yarn into the first incision along the bottom edge.

9. Loop it behind the loom and bring the yarn forward through the second incision along the bottom edge. Run the yarn up and over the top edge, pressing it into the second incision along the top edge.

10. Loop the yarn behind the loom and bring it over the top edge again, pressing the yarn into the third incision. Continue warping this way all along the loom. When you have reached the last incision, secure the end behind the loom with another piece of masking tape.

To Weave:

1. Start with a piece of yarn about 24" long in your first desired color. (If you want to use all one color, you'll still need to weave with smaller lengths of yarn. Don't use a piece longer than about 36".) Thread the plastic needle. Don't bother with a knot.

2. You can start on either side. Slide the needle under the first thread, over the second, under the third, and so on to the end of the row. Leave about 4" of the end of the yarn sticking out the beginning of the row.

3. For the second row, bring the needle around the outermost warp thread, then go over and under the warp threads to the other side. Make sure you're going over the threads you went under in the first row and vice versa. Don't pull the yarn too tight at the end of the row, otherwise you'll end up pulling the outermost warp threads toward the center. (These outermost threads are called the *selvedges*.)

4. Repeat these two rows. After every four or five rows, take the fork or wide-toothed comb and gently push the weft threads down toward the base of the loom. Don't pack them down too hard; just neaten them up so the rows lie barely touching one another.

5. You can change color any time you like by slipping the needle off the current yarn at the beginning or end of a row, leaving the last few inches draped off to the side, and starting a new length of yarn in the color of your choice. If you want to keep using the same color, make sure you leave those few inches of the original length of yarn off to the side, and start a new length, leaving a few inches of the new piece of yarn sticking out to the side as well. (You'll deal with these ends sticking out later.)

6. Continue until you have woven all the way up the warp yarn to the top of the loom.

Finishing:

1. Start weaving in the loose ends. Thread the needle with one of the ends and weave it carefully into the yarn woven around it. Make sure you loop the end around a warp thread first so that you don't accidentally unweave the yarn. You can trim the loose end after you've woven it back into the fabric for an inch or two. Do this for each loose end.

2. Take one of the twigs or craft sticks and start lifting loops off the top of the woven piece, one at a time, and slip them onto the stick. If the loops are too loose or the stick too thin, add another stick along the first one and tie the ends together with yarn from your project. (You could also glue them together after you've woven the second stick through; avoid getting glue on your weaving.)

3. Repeat along the bottom with the other twig or craft stick.

4. To hang, cut a piece of yarn about 10" long and tie it to either end of the top stick.

Tips:

- You can sew or tie beads, pompoms, or other items onto the fabric either as you go or after the weaving is complete.
- If this craft interests you, there are wooden frame looms, like the cardboard one you made for this project, that are commercially available.

Clay Offering-Bowl Craft

This craft makes a small offering bowl, about 3" in diameter. An offering bowl is used to hold offerings to an entity or abstract. Offerings can be as simple as a flower or some water or whatever you feel will be pleasing.

Working with clay can be immensely rewarding. It's a way to connect to the element of earth, and the cool damp feeling can be relaxing, while the pressure and force needed to shape it can be satisfying. The clay you choose is up to you. Your local art-supply shop can offer a variety of clay: clay that can air dry or clay that can be baked in the oven. Please follow the directions on the packaging of the clay you choose for working with and finishing the clay.

What You Need:

- Plastic gloves (optional)
- Clay (air-dry clay is recommended)
- Newspaper

What to Do:

1. Put on the gloves, if using. Cover your working surface with newspaper.
2. Pinch off a knob of clay about 4" in diameter and shape it into a ball.
3. Push your thumb down into the middle. Don't press it all the way through to the other side.
4. Start pinching the edges to make the sides of the bowl. Gently pull the sides out at the top to make a gentle outward slope.
5. Shape or smooth the bottom of the dish as well.
6. If desired, draw designs into the inside or outside of the dish (see following tips).
7. Allow the dish to air dry.

Tips:

+ Painting the clay before it dries can create a crackle effect; however, depending on the paint and clay combo, it can also flake off. The type of paint you use will depend on what type of clay you've chosen to work with. Research what paints are most suitable. Experiment with some scrap clay first.
+ You can carefully pinch or shape the upper edge of the bowl to make a fluted or not-round shape.
+ For this basic craft, you don't need any specific tools. However, if you wish to make designs on the bowl, you can use toothpicks, a small screwdriver, a dried-out ballpoint pen, and/or the like. If you repurpose something from the household that you'll need to use again, make sure to wash it well to avoid clay drying in any small grooves.

Chapter 5

Household Self-Care

Your home is your spiritual retreat. You start from it every morning and come back to it at night, and the energy of the space should reflect the protection, nurturing, and support you need from it. Maintaining the energy of your home in the best possible alignment benefits you and anyone who uses the space. That means cleansing or purifying it regularly, protecting it with energy barriers to defend it against unwanted energies, and working to keep it in physical shape as well.

Create Comfort

Surrounding yourself with things that bring you comfort helps you release tension. The idea of an environment that supports and nurtures you is one that magic encourages. Creating a magical environment with energy that supports your goals is a very common practice for a witch. It's also an excellent approach for self-care. Programming the energy of your environment to nurture your spirit adds an extra layer on top of decorating your space with things that bring you joy.

First of all, examine your space. What about it do you like? What frustrates you? Is there anything in it that you associate with bad memories? Are there any elements that make you feel odd or downright bad? Make note of them. Remove them if you can.

Think about the vision for your room(s). What would you like to see more of that is already there? What would you like to include that isn't there? Is there anything you would like to deliberately place in it to bring in specific energy?

A busy room may make you happy. If so, examine why. Is it because it's distracting? Does it help you dodge thinking about things? That may be avoidance, which is not healthy in the long run. It can provide a kind of vacation and break from the daily grind, but avoidance isn't a sustainable coping mechanism.

Think about what you can add that would bring you peace. Is it more of a specific color, a texture? What could you take away to improve how you feel in the room?

Cluttered Space, Cluttered Energy

Something you need to think about is clutter. It can be daunting to sort through it, but clutter left in a space that is supposed to be calming works against the purpose. Even if you don't notice it consciously, clutter is a stress that impacts you. You can even start accepting it as part of the space if it is there too long, which isn't what you want at all.

Reduce the amount of stuff. That can be hard if you're a pack rat or if you love collecting. If that's the case, think about organizing in such a way that creates harmony instead of visual clutter. But packing a lot into a small space is a recipe for tension. Reduce what you can. A riot of color can also be visually stressful.

Daily Maintenance

At the end of each day walk through each room and do a quick tidy. Encourage other members of your family to do the same. Light, ongoing maintenance is much easier to do than putting a drastic time investment into overhauling a room. (Remember, self-care is about making things easier and less stressful for yourself!)

Elemental Balancing

The four classical elements are earth, air, fire, and water. Each has a specific kind of energy to it. Many people often have an affinity for one or more elements and find the associated energy soothing.

Very basically, the elemental energies are:

- Earth: stability, firm, grounded, prosperity
- Air: light, adaptability, clear thought
- Fire: passionate, activity, change
- Water: purifying, fluid, transformation, healing

A good exercise is to spend time in a room and open yourself to its energy. How does it feel? Does it tend strongly toward one element?

Working with elemental energy in a home can involve looking to correct an imbalance of energy (controlling the overpresence of an element by introducing other elemental energy) or to encourage the presence of an element in order to enhance the desired feeling in a room. For example, a bedroom should be soothing and calm in order to encourage proper rest. An excess of air or fire energy would not be conducive to that.

If you have an excess of energy related to one element, try to balance it with the energy of another element with more conducive energy to cancel it out. For example, if you have too much air energy in your bedroom, don't add fire energy; instead, reach for earth energy. You could use water energy as well, but think about the ultimate goal of your room and go with the energy that feels the most appropriate.

How do you go about introducing elemental energy?

- **Color** is an easy way to do it. Think about your emotional response to colors and choose one or two that reinforce the type of energy you are looking for. Another way to choose color is to look at traditional energy associations for colors (red being associated with passion and activity, blue being associated with peace and protection, green being associated with health and abundance, and so forth) and pull in one or two that resonate with the energy you're looking for. Try the emotional response first, though; your response to color is more valid for your purposes than general lists.

- **Plants** bring earth energy. They also have the added bonus of cleaning the air and providing positive energy in general. Stay on top of caring for them, however; dead plants have the opposite effect.

- **Crystals and stones** carry their own native energy as well as being excellent vehicles for energy you program into them. They are associated with earth energy in general, but each stone has its own energy that you can draw on to help balance the energy of a room. If the room feels less positive or supportive than you wish it to be, try placing rose quartz in it to transform negative energy into positive energy. Use a chunk of amethyst to create a feeling of peace, and so forth.

Cleansing and Purifying

Maintenance of your home's energy should be a priority. Fortunately, it's easy to do. As mentioned, crystals and houseplants can be used to passively and constantly purify your space on a low level, but you'll need to do a larger, more active clearing of negative energy on a regular basis in order to keep your space in the best shape possible to support your self-care.

Here are some ways to cleanse the energy of your home:

- Sweep with a broom, visualizing negative energy being broken up and swept away.
- Burn a sage smudge, a small bundle of dried sage tied together. Sage is excellent for banishing negative energy.
- Use a purifying mist or a cleansing powder like the following.

Purifying Mist

Use this simple spray to help purify areas of your home.

What You Need:

- 1 cup distilled water
- Spray bottle
- ¼ teaspoon salt
- 10 drops sandalwood essential oil
- 8 drops frankincense essential oil
- 6 drops lavender essential oil
- 4 drops rose essential-oil blend

What to Do:

1. Pour the water into the spray bottle. Add the salt and swirl to dissolve and combine.
2. Add the essential oils and shake gently to combine.
3. To use, set the spray bottle to a mist and mist the room you wish to purify or in which you wish to eliminate negative energy.

Cleansing Powder

Powders are sprinkled through an area to spread their magical energies around to do their work. Afterward, they are swept or vacuumed up. In this blend, salt is the heavy lifter in terms of purifying, supported by the cleansing and also protective and blessing qualities of the rosemary and sage, and the positive energy of the rose. Technically it's not a powder, because the salt isn't ground to powder, but no one's going to stop you from calling it that. (For a true powder, use cornstarch in place of the salt. You'll lose the purification properties of the salt, although the rest of the ingredients still carry that energy.)

What You Need:

+ 3 tablespoons fine salt
+ Small bowl
+ 1 teaspoon dried sage
+ 1 teaspoon dried rose petals
+ 1 teaspoon dried rosemary

What to Do:

1. Place the salt in the bowl.
2. Crumble the dried herbs into the salt, making the particles of herbs as small as possible. (If you have a mortar and pestle, use it to grind the dried herbs first.)
3. Use your fingers to mix the herbs and salt together. Pause with your fingers in the blend and say, *"Powder, I charge you to cleanse and purify the energy of the place in which you are sprinkled. So may it be."*
4. Take pinches of the blend and sprinkle it around the area you want to cleanse. Allow it to rest there for about an hour or overnight. Sweep it up with a broom and dustpan the next day, or vacuum it up. Dispose of the powder or contents of the vacuum in an outside bin.

Tip:

♦ This is a great method to adapt for whatever magical purpose you like. Using salt or cornstarch as the base, you can include whatever herbs resonate with the energy of your goal.

Music

One of the ways you can affect the energy of your home and also impact your self-care is by playing music. Chapter 4 looked at how playing music can affect the emotional and creative aspects of self-care. Music can also be used to affect the energy of a space.

Sounds waves are energy that moves. Harnessing that energy to have an effect on the energy of a space is easy to do.

If you are looking to break up negative or stagnant energy in a space, you can use drums, maracas, or clap your hands sharply. Move through the space you're working in, remembering to reach into corners and spaces where energy doesn't circulate well.

If you want to settle slightly out-of-sync energy or calm energy that is a bit too antsy, look into using a Tibetan singing bowl, a metal bowl that creates a sustained note when a mallet is lightly run around the rim. Running a finger around the damp rim of a wine glass can be a substitute in a pinch, but nothing beats the rich, complex layers of a real singing bowl. Bells are also common instruments to enhance or calm the energy of a space. Use a single bell and ring it throughout the room, allowing time between the rings to let the vibrations flow.

Wind chimes also work to break up negativity or to create positive energy, depending on the size and tuning of them. The deeper ones tend to be good for turning away or breaking up negativity, but the lighter, higher-pitched ones seem to work well inside for calming energy or uplifting the energy that is already pleasant.

Chanting can also work to transform negative energy to positive energy. A chant that is commonly used is the om mantra, but feel free to search out other chants on the Internet to learn them. If you sing them yourself, it has the added bonus of positively affecting your personal vibration. If you prefer to play a recording, that's fine, but the effect will be slightly different.

Protecting Your Home's Energy

Once you're regularly purifying your home, doesn't it make sense to protect its energy so you don't have to do so much spiritual housework? Keep the negative energy out as much as possible, and your home will feel much safer, enabling you to relax more.

There are several easy ways to defend your home's energy:

• Plant shrubs or plants associated with protection around it, such as juniper, peonies, ivy, and basil.

• Hang a braid of onions or garlic in the house to absorb negative energy. (Don't eat these! Compost them after a year and buy a new braid.)

• Draw a protective symbol under your welcome mat with a Sharpie marker.

• Draw protective symbols on your windows with salt water. Do the same over your doorways and around the locks on your doors.

• Place stones with protective qualities around the house, such as obsidian, onyx, and amethyst.

Enhancing Home Energy Pillar Candle

One of the easiest self-care actions is to light a candle. There is something soothing about initiating light; flame is a living thing, and the light it casts is warm. This spell shows you how to prepare a regular pillar candle dedicated to self-care, using a technique called *loading*. It uses powdered herbs and oils as well as carved words. These techniques can be applied to other kinds of candles as well; feel free to experiment. Use this candle to enhance the restorative, supportive energy of your home. This technique can be used for other magical purposes; simply tailor the herbs, oils, and stone to your goal.

What You Need:

- Pillar candle
- Ice pick, metal skewer (single-point), or long nail
- Matches or lighter
- Tea light candle
- Pinch dried lavender
- Pinch dried chamomile
- Pinch dried rose petals
- Mortar and pestle
- Sandalwood essential oil
- Small chip of rose quartz
- Candleholder or base

What to Do:

1. Center and ground.
2. Turn the pillar candle upside down.
3. Light the tea light and hold the pointy end of the ice pick, skewer, or nail in the flame to heat the metal. When the metal is hot, gently push it into the bottom of the candle parallel to the wick to make a deep hole. (Don't insert it right along the wick; leave wax between the wick and the hole you're making.) If you like, you can reheat the metal and insert it into the candle again to enlarge the hole for ease of loading the candle.
4. Place the dried herbs in the mortar. Use the pestle to grind them into a powder, as finely as possible. Add a drop of sandalwood oil and use the pestle to mix it into the herbs.
5. Carefully pick up pinches of the herb blend and gently poke them into the hole. Tweezers may help, or you may prefer to enlarge the hole some more. When you have filled the hole, press the chip of rose quartz into the hole. To seal it, drip a bit of the liquid wax from the original tea light over the stone chip, or hold a match or lighter close to (not touching) the wax around the hole.
6. To use, make sure the pillar candle is in a candleholder or on a base of some kind.

Altars and Shrines

Altars and shrines can both be useful tools in spiritual self-care. They serve to provide a place in the home where you can touch base with the Divine or nourish your spiritual state. There tends to be confusion between them, though. What's the difference between the two?

♦ An altar is a work space or focus for worship.

♦ A shrine is a small collection of objects assembled to honor or enhance a focus.

Altars are often used for active worship of a deity. Whereas a shrine honors something or someone, an altar is an active—or interactive!—interface for religious worship or prayer.

Creating a Gratitude Shrine

This shrine provides a semipermanent place to express gratitude for the good things in your life. It also serves the purpose of reminding you to be grateful, reminding you of all the blessings you enjoy. This can be a key strategy in fighting the day-to-day tendency to be affected by the things that go wrong. Seeing your Gratitude Shrine should uplift you.

The supplies listed are suggestions. If other things call to you— shells, photos, animal figurines, origami animals—by all means, use them in constructing your Gratitude Shrine.

What You Need:

- Small cloth or tray
- Card with affirmation or inspirational quote on it
- Rose quartz stone
- Clear quartz stone
- Matches or lighter
- Votive candle (color of your choice) and candleholder

What to Do:

1. Choose a space that can be easily accessed and seen but not right in the middle of activity so that it doesn't get torn apart while someone looks for their keys. Look for a flat, protected surface.
2. Lay down a small cloth or tray.
3. Arrange your objects pleasingly on it. Set the candle in the candleholder in a safe spot.
4. To use, center and ground, light the candle, and say something such as,

    Great Universe,
    Thank you for my many blessings.
    I thank you for the food I eat,
    The roof over my head,
    The comforts I enjoy,
    The family that supports me,
    The friends who love me,
    And the health I enjoy.
    May I always be grateful for these blessings and all others.

5. You can also write things you're grateful for on slips of paper and leave them at the gratitude shrine.
6. Every once in a while, put a small glass of water, wine, or other drink at the shrine as another way of showing appreciation.

Tips:

- A small wall shelf can also be used for a gratitude shrine.
- Add a few drops of essential oil to the candle by burning it until there is a small pool of liquid wax, extinguishing the candle, adding the drops to the liquid wax, then relighting the candle.

Creating a Shadowbox Shrine

This shrine is constructed in a small wooden box that can be opened and closed. Ideally you can open it and stand it up on its small end. Depending on the size, it might be possible to travel with it. If the box is deep enough, you might even be able to place figurines on the base inside the box.

What You Need:

- Small items such as costume jewelry, dried flowers, silk flowers, scrapbook stickers, sequins, beads, shells, and so on
- Small pictures cut from magazines or printed out from the Internet
- Hinged wooden box from a craft store (shallow; not too deep)
- Acrylic paints and paintbrushes
- Glitter glue
- Glue
- Mod Podge sealer
- Foam brush

What to Do:

1. Consider what you want this shrine to be dedicated to. Happiness and joy? Peace and harmony? Collect small items that represent your theme with which to decorate the box shrine.

2. Set the wooden box in front of you so that the hinges are on the left. Unlatch it and open it like a book. Then tilt it toward you so that it stands up on the smaller end, the lid still open to the left like the cover of a book.

3. Plan out how you will paint the box. Paint it and allow it to dry. (Remember that you can paint the exterior of the box as well!)

4. While the paint dries, take some time to position your items in a pleasing arrangement that is meaningful to you. Remember that you can fill all the walls of the box, not just the bottom/back wall of the box shrine and the inner lid.

5. Transfer the arrangement to the box piece by piece, gluing them down. Decorate with glitter glue, if desired. When dry, apply Mod Podge with the foam brush to seal it all.

Creating an Altar to Yourself

You may be uncomfortable with the idea of worshipping yourself or not feel you're worth worshipping. That should change! Everyone has a spark of the Divine inside them. That is worth honoring. You are worth honoring as a vessel of the Divine as well.

Collect things that you associate with yourself. Photos you love, jewelry, trinkets; things you may not use anymore but still love fall into this category. Items from your childhood are great to use as well, if they remind you of happy times. Favorite books? Favorite colors? Draw them all in to help assemble this self-care space to honor you.

Choose a place to set up your altar. A small wall shelf somewhere is a great idea, if you want to keep it small and simple. You can hang pictures or art on the wall above or around it. Decorate it however you like: add shells, drape scarves, add action figures... This is for you. Make sure there's room for a candle. A votive in a glass candleholder taller than the candle is a good idea, to protect the things around it from the flame.

What You Need:

- Framed photo of yourself (size of your choice)
- Representations of your activities (job, hobbies, and so on)
- Representations of life events (such as rites of passage, medals, trophies, and so on)
- 2–3 of your favorite stones or crystals
- Candle (color of your choice) and candleholder
- Matches or lighter

What to Do:

1. Assemble your chosen items where you've chosen to set up your altar. Set the candle in the middle and arrange the other objects around them.
2. As you place them, take a moment to remember how proud or happy you felt at each life stage or achievement. Appreciate how hard you work at your job. Feel gratitude for your hobbies. As you build the altar to yourself, build the feeling of pride and love for yourself and the person you are.
3. When the altar is complete, center and ground. Light the candle. Look slowly and deliberately at the items you have collected and displayed.

4. Say:

> *I honor myself.*
> *I honor my strength.*
> *I honor my past that has led me here.*
> *I honor my skills, my talents.*
> *I honor my determination.*
> *I honor my need for space and time to myself.*
> *I honor my rights.*
> *I honor my potential.*

5. When you are done, you can extinguish the candle.
6. At least once a week, return to the altar and light the candle. Let your gaze travel over your collection that makes up the altar and be proud of who you are. Repeat the prayer above, if you like. Go to the altar when you feel worn out, are fighting low self-esteem, or doubting your awesomeness.

Tip:

◆ This altar is by no means static. It's a work in progress. Add to it as often as you like.

Aromatherapy

As a way to control stress and uplift mood, aromatherapy is a terrific tool in your self-care arsenal. Spellcraft often pulls aromatherapy in as a secondary element; the primary use of oils and herbs is for their energies, of course. But it's a pleasant bonus when your blends smell good as well.

Scent is one of the strongest memory triggers. No wonder; despite its apparent intangibility, scent is inescapable and deeply tied to emotion. The scent receptors (on the olfactory nerve) are positioned right next to the amygdala and the hippocampus, the emotional centers of the brain.

Aromatherapy uses plants, flowers, or the extracted oils to positively affect your physiological or physical state. The gist of the science is that certain compounds stimulate different areas of the brain or the production of mood-affecting neurotransmitters. It's generally safe, although care should be taken when working with essential oils to not allow them to touch your eyes or the inside of the nose, and certain oils (such as cinnamon) shouldn't be applied directly to the skin because of the potential for irritation. Essential oils generally shouldn't be taken orally, either; drinking them can damage your liver or kidneys. Only do so if a qualified medical professional approves it after reviewing your current state of health, prescriptions, and over-the-counter medications. Ingesting them can be especially dangerous because essential oils aren't regulated the way medicine is; there is no way to confirm if the oil is what it says it is on the label, with no additives. Consult a reliable guide to educate yourself on the guidelines and handling of specific essential oils, such as Roberta Wilson's *Aromatherapy: Essential Oils for Vibrant Health and Beauty.*

> Store your essential oils and oil blends in a dark place to keep the components from breaking down or going bad.

Common applications of essential oils include diluting them in water and heating them in a diffuser or spraying the diluted solution in the air, and diluting the essential oil in a carrier oil such as sweet almond, jojoba, or grapeseed oil and rubbing it on the skin. A simple, efficient method is to place a drop of oil on a cotton ball and place it in a zip-top bag. Carry it with you through the day, unzipping the bag to breathe in the scent when you need it.

Here are a few essential oils that are particularly useful in the practice of self-care. The magical and physical benefits are rolled into one.

- Clary Sage: Clary sage essential oil is used for optimism, happiness, relaxation, antianxiety, and confidence.
- Frankincense: Frankincense essential oil is used for meditation, clarity, and purification. The woody scent is slightly spicy.
- Jasmine: Jasmine essential oil is used for meditation, clarity, and self-love. The scent is floral but clean; it has a green undertone.
- Lavender: As detailed in earlier chapters, lavender is a wonderful self-care oil and herb. It's used for relaxation with a sedative effect, for calm and sleep.
- Lemon: Lemon essential oil is used for happiness, clarity, joy, and purification.
- Sandalwood: A sweet woody scent, sandalwood is often used in spiritual traditions. Sandalwood essential oil is used for meditation, relaxation without a sedative effect, purification, calm, and clarity.
- Ylang-Ylang: A sweet floral oil, ylang-ylang is used for relaxation and serenity.

Aromatherapy Blends for Self-Care

There are a variety of ways to incorporate aromatherapy into your self-care. The quickest and easiest way is to directly apply a dot of the blended oil onto your inner wrist so that the scent and any physical benefits of the oils are immediately available to you. There are various forms of jewelry that carry scent, such as locket-type pendants or bracelets made of lava stone, a porous substance that absorbs drops of oil placed on it and slowly releases the scent through the day.

> Essential oils are very concentrated, which is why they're usually diluted in a carrier oil such as sweet almond oil, jojoba oil, or grapeseed oil if you're going to be using them on the skin. Diffusion doesn't always require a carrier oil, so if you're mixing a blend for this kind of diffusion (in other words, if you're *not* going to be applying it to the skin) then you can omit the carrier oil in whatever recipe you're following. Make sure you label your blend and note if it includes a carrier oil!

Diffusion is the process by which an oil is dispersed throughout an area. There are several ways to do this.

- Putting drops on a cotton ball and tucking it into a tiny zip-top bag allows you to carry it with you. Open the bag and bring it to your face, inhaling deeply. This is a great method to bring a blend with you on a plane or to work.

- You can add drops of oil to a small bottle of distilled water. Shake it, then spray it on sofas, beds, carpets, or just into the air to add fragrance to the room.

- Diffusion via steam is another simple method. Boil 1–2 cups water, transfer it to a bowl, and add drops of the oil to the water. The heat of the water will disperse the aroma through the area. (You may be familiar with this method if you've ever draped a towel over your head and a bowl of steaming water—with or without a drop or two of eucalyptus oil—to help loosen congestion; boiled cinnamon sticks, cloves, and orange peel at Christmas will make the house smell cozy.)

- A candle diffuser is a small dish on top of a candleholder. Place a tablespoon or two of water into the dish and add drops of oil to it. The candle heats the water and oils, and the scent is released into the air. An electric diffuser does the same thing, only it uses electricity to heat the dish.

- A nebulizer breaks down the oils into smaller particles and diffuses them into the air. Nebulizers are also powered by an electric pump.

- A lovely, relaxing way to enjoy aromatherapy is in a bath. You can add a few drops of your chosen blend directly to the water after you have filled your bath, or mix them into a larger amount of carrier oil to make a bath oil. (See Chapter 3 for bath oil recipes.)

Here are some magical blends that you can use in a diffuser, aromatherapy jewelry, or to dab on squares of cloth and tuck in various places.

Some of these blends call for oils that weren't previously listed. If so, the associated magical properties are mentioned in the recipe.

Gentle Sleep Oil

Place a dot of this blend on each temple and underside of the wrist before bed, or dab a bit on the edge of your bed near your pillow. Makes about 1 ounce.

What You Need:

- 1 tablespoon carrier oil
- 10 drops lavender essential oil
- 8 drops sandalwood essential oil
- 5 drops ylang-ylang essential oil
- 1-ounce glass bottle with cap
- Label and pen or marker

What to Do:

1. Center and ground.
2. Mix the carrier oil and the other oil drops together in a small bottle, focusing on the goal of peaceful sleep as you do. Cap the bottle and hold it between your hands, saying, *"I charge you to bring restful sleep. May rest be deep, may I wake refreshed. So may it be."*
3. Label the bottle.

Happy House Oil

This is a terrific blend to use in a diffuser. Sweet orange and bergamot essential oils carry energies associated with happiness and health. This blend also vibrates with energies associated with purification. Makes about 1 ounce.

What You Need:

- 1 tablespoon carrier oil
- 8 drops lemon essential oil
- 8 drops sweet orange essential oil
- 8 drops bergamot essential oil
- 8 drops sandalwood or frankincense essential oil
- 1-ounce glass bottle with cap
- Label and pen or marker

What to Do:

1. Center and ground.
2. Mix the carrier oil and other oil drops together in a small bottle, focusing on the goal of a happy house as you do. Cap the bottle and hold it between your hands, saying, *"I charge you to bring joyful vibrations to this home, that all who live and visit may be happy. So may it be."*
3. Label the bottle.

Mindfulness Oil Blend

This helps you focus on the immediate moment instead of getting your head stuck in the past or worrying about the future. Makes 1 ounce.

What You Need:

- 1 tablespoon carrier oil
- 10 drops frankincense essential oil
- 10 drops sandalwood essential oil
- 5 drops jasmine essential oil
- 5 drops clary sage essential oil
- 1-ounce glass bottle with cap
- Label and pen or marker

What to Do:

1. Center and ground.
2. Mix the carrier oil and other oil drops together in a small bottle, focusing on the goal of mindfulness as you do. Cap the bottle and hold it between your hands, saying, *"I charge you to help keep my mind in the present, focused on the here and now. So may it be."*
3. Label the bottle.

Incense

Incense is a blend of herbs and/or resins that is placed on a piece of smoldering charcoal in a censer or other heatproof dish to release scent and energy. Incense can be an offering, a way to produce energy sympathetic or supportive to a specific goal or purpose, or simply something to enjoy.

Here are some general notes about incense:

- Make sure you have about one part resin to one part green matter. It lasts longer while burning, and the resin has a sweetness that balances the more acrid smell of the herbal matter.

- You can add a few drops of essential oil to your incense blend, but no more than a few; saturating the herbal matter isn't recommended. Toss the mixture after adding the drops of oil, then put it in a container and seal it to keep the scent until you need to use the incense.

- Loose incense is burned on charcoal tablets sold for that purpose, available at ethnic grocery stores, New Age shops, or ecclesiastical supply stores. Hold the tablet with a pair of tweezers or small tongs and hold a flame to the edge. The charcoal will catch, and a series of small red sparks will run across it. After a short while the surface of the charcoal will begin to glow red. Lay the tablet down gently on a bed of sand, fine gravel, or a metal mesh in a heatproof bowl. When the tablet glows, take a pinch of your incense blend and sprinkle it on the charcoal. Smoke will begin to rise.

- Less is more. Too much incense on the tablet can smother it or produce a staggering amount of smoke that you'll have to deal with by opening windows to air out the room.
- Always have a small fire extinguisher, bottle of water, or bowl of sand nearby to put out the charcoal if necessary.

Incense Blends

Most of these use frankincense or copal as the resin component. Frankincense is an excellent all-purpose resin that possesses energies related to healing, purification, blessing, meditation, serenity, protection, love, and blessing. Golden copal is associated with purification, clearing blockages, blessing, joy, uplifting your mood, and fighting depression.

There are different kinds of copal. Use the yellow copal, sometimes called golden copal (*Protium copal*). White copal (*Shorea javanica*) can also be used, but it tends to be more expensive.

To blend incense:

- Use a stone mortar and pestle to gently crush the resin if it is not in small granules. Don't grind too hard or the resin will start to melt and become gummy. Think of cracking the resins instead. Transfer the resins to a small jar or other container.
- Separately, grind the dried herbs, or rub them between your fingers to crumble them. Add any drops of essential oil to the dried herbs, stir, then add the herbs to the container with the resins.
- Cap and shake gently to combine.
- Use ½ teaspoon incense at a time, no more.

Serenity Incense

- 9–12 drops jasmine essential oil
- 1 teaspoon frankincense resin
- 1 teaspoon copal resin
- 2 teaspoons white sandalwood powder

Grounding Incense

- 1 teaspoon patchouli
- 1 teaspoon sandalwood (red)
- 2 teaspoons myrrh resin
- 1 drop vanilla extract

Joy Incense

- 1 teaspoon dried lemon zest
- 1 teaspoon dried orange zest
- 9–12 drops bergamot essential oil
- 2 teaspoons copal resin
- ½ teaspoon ground ginger

Peace Incense

- 9 drops gardenia or ylang-ylang essential oil
- 1 teaspoon dried lavender
- 1 teaspoon dried rose petals
- 2 teaspoons frankincense resin

Healing Incense

- 1 teaspoon amber
- 1 teaspoon copal resin
- 1 teaspoon dried lemon zest
- 1 teaspoon dried orange zest

Bibliography

Brown, Brené. *The Gifts of Imperfection: Let Go of Who You Think You're Supposed to Be and Embrace Who You Are.* Center City, MN: Hazelden Publishing, 2010.

Cirillo, Francesco. "The Pomodoro Technique." https://francescocirillo.com/pages/pomodoro-technique. Accessed May 29, 2018.

Cunningham, Scott. *Cunningham's Encyclopedia of Wicca in the Kitchen.* 3rd ed. St. Paul, MN: Llewellyn, 2003.

Gilbert, Elizabeth. *Big Magic: Creative Living Beyond Fear.* London: Bloomsbury, 2015.

Hauck, Carley. "4 Questions to Foster Your Authentic Self." Mindful.org. October 12, 2016. www.mindful.org/4-questions-foster-authentic-self/. Accessed May 7, 2018.

Hoffman, Rachel. "Unfuck Your Habitat." *Tumblr.* May 2, 2018, 7:12 a.m. (No subject header.) http://unfuckyourhabitat.tumblr.com/post/173510795531/depression-anxiety-addadhd-executive-function. Accessed May 2, 2018.

———. *Unfuck Your Habitat: You're Better Than Your Mess.* New York: St. Martin's/Griffin, 2017.

Janssen, Mary Beth. *The Book of Self-Care: Remedies for Healing Mind, Body, and Soul.* New York: Sterling, 2017.

Linn, Denise. *Altars: Bringing Sacred Shrines Into Your Everyday Life.* New York: Ballantine Wellspring, 1999.

Morrison, Dorothy. *Everyday Magic: Spells & Rituals for Modern Living*. St. Paul, MN: Llewellyn, 1998.

Murphy-Hiscock, Arin. *The Green Witch: Your Complete Guide to the Natural Magic of Herbs, Flowers, Essential Oils, and More*. Avon, MA: Adams Media, 2017.

———. *The House Witch: Your Complete Guide to Creating a Magical Space with Rituals and Spells for Hearth and Home*. Avon, MA: Adams Media, 2018.

———. *Power Spellcraft for Life: The Art of Crafting and Casting for Positive Change*. Avon, MA: Adams Media, 2005.

———. *Protection Spells: Clear Negative Energy, Banish Unhealthy Influences, and Embrace Your Power*. Avon, MA: Adams Media, 2018.

———. *Solitary Wicca for Life: A Complete Guide to Mastering the Craft on Your Own*. Avon, MA: Adams Media, 2005.

Norville, Andrea, and Patrick Menton. *An Indulgence a Day: 365 Simple Ways to Spoil Yourself*. Avon, MA: Adams Media, 2009.

O'Hara, Gwydion. *The Magick of Aromatherapy: The Use of Scent for Healing Body, Mind, and Spirit*. St. Paul, MN: Llewellyn, 1998.

Wiking, Meik. *The Little Book of Hygge: The Danish Way to Live Well*. London: Penguin, 2016.

Wilson, Roberta. *Aromatherapy: Essential Oils for Vibrant Health and Beauty*. Revised and updated ed. New York: Avery, 2002.

Index